Deanna & Robert,
Best Wishes for a lifetime
of Love and Happiness! I
hope you enjoy this book.
Congratulations!
Maria Francisco
2-1-2020

ROBERT & DEANNA,
    ENJOY! MARIA IS OUR GREAT FRIEND WE KNOW IN RINCON P.R.
They LIVE LONG BRANCH, N.J. & RINCON FUN HOME!
2-22-20
♡♡
            ♡ SEARS CREW!
            DON, KIM, KATE, LIZ, BARBARA, HOBIE

DEDICATION

I dedicate this cookbook to my family and friends that I've had the pleasure of cooking for in the past 25 years. Whether it was a dinner with a large group or a chicken cutlet sandwich on a flight we shared, food brings us all together. So many memories were made, dining on delicious meals, sharing good wine & great company!

Buon Appetito!

ACKNOWLEDGMENTS

Special thanks to my beautiful daughter Gina who inspired me to put all of my recipes together in this book. I want to also thank my mama, Rosaria, Sicilian born, who cooked delicious meals for us every day and who taught me the love of good food and the importance of fresh ingredients.

Maria Francisco

CONTENTS

Arancini
Bacon Wrapped Scallops
Barbeque Pizza on the Grill
Bruschetta
Caponata
Eggplant Parmigiana
Empanadillas
Figs Stuffed with Gorgonzola
Popovers
Steamed Dumplings
Stuffed Mushrooms
Sushi Rolls
Zucchini Flowers

Appetizers

ARANCINI
(Rice Balls)
Yields 12-15 Rice Balls

3 cups arborio rice
1 tbsp. saffron
6 cups chicken stock
½ pound ground beef
3 eggs
¼ cup olive oil
½ onion, finely chopped
¼ cup peas

1 cup tomato sauce
1 tsp. salt
¼ tsp. black pepper
1 cup grated parmigiano
2 cups unseasoned breadcrumbs
1 cup flour
vegetable oil for frying

*Prepare rice a few hours ahead or overnight.

Prepare the Rice:
In a large pot, bring stock to a boil and add the rice. Cook over medium heat, stirring frequently for 20-25 minutes until liquid has been absorbed.

Dissolve the saffron in ¼ cup hot water and stir into the rice along with the parmigiana cheese. Stir well and leave to cool for 5 minutes, then add 1 beaten egg, mix well and refrigerate, covered, for at least 2 hours or overnight preferred.

Prepare the Meat Stuffing:
In a sauté pan, sauté the onion in olive oil for few minutes until translucent, add meat and brown meat until cooked. Drain the fat and add peas and tomato sauce, salt and pepper and continue to simmer for another 15 minutes. Put aside and let cool.

Form the rice into balls, about the size of a small orange. Make a deep depression in the center with your thumb (the size of a walnut) and fill with meat mixture, then seal the opening with more rice so the meat is in the center. Beat two eggs in a bowl to make an egg bath. Dust the rice ball in flour seasoned with salt and pepper and roll first in the egg bath then in breadcrumbs.

Heat the oil in a deep pan about 1/3 of the way up. When oil is very hot, fry the rice balls a few at a time until golden. Drain on paper towels.

BACON WRAPPED SCALLOPS
Serves 6

24 fresh sea scallops

12 slices of bacon

8 tbsp. butter

3 garlic cloves

dash of cayenne pepper

24 toothpicks

Preheat oven to 400 degrees.

Cut bacon slices in half and precook just a bit.

Grease a baking pan.

In a small pan, melt butter, add garlic, and a dash of cayenne. Put half of the mixture in a bowl and set the remainder aside for later.

The scallop tends to have a small fleshy tab, about the size of a fingernail, on its side. This tab should be peeled off, as it is tougher than the rest of the scallop. Dip each scallop in the butter mixture, then wrap bacon around scallop and secure with a toothpick through the scallop. Arrange on baking dish, don't over crowd.

Bake 10-15 minutes until crisp. Put on serving plate, pour the rest of the butter over the scallops and serve.

BARBEQUE PIZZA ON THE GRILL
Serves 8

2 pizza doughs (fresh or frozen)	ham chopped
tomato sauce -see page 59	anchovies
condiments:	blue cheese
shredded mozzarella	goat cheese
mushrooms	½ cup olive oil
pepperoni slices	salt and pepper to taste
fresh sliced tomatoes with basil	paint brush or pastry brush

Place your choice of condiments from above (or choose your own) in small bowls, about 1 cup of each. In another bowl, mix the olive oil, salt and pepper. Keep the paint brush close by to baste the dough.

Heat barbeque grill 10 minutes prior to about 350 degrees (medium heat). Using a large cutting board as work area, dust the cutting board with a little flour, then cut the pizza dough in half, work it and stretch it out as thin as you can without putting a hole through it. Use a rolling pin (or a wine bottle) if you'd like.

Once dough is stretched out, use a brush and oil on one side of the dough, then lift and place the oiled side facing down on the grill, wait 2 minutes. Then baste the raw side of the dough with the oil, let cook for few minutes, lift a corner to check. When dough looks cooked on one side, flip it over.

Immediately add and spread the tomato sauce, toppings, and mozzarella. Then close the grill lid and let the cheese melt. When the bottom of the pizza looks cooked, remove to a serving plate. Let cool for 5 minutes, then serve.

BRUSCHETTA
Serves 8

1 baguette – sliced ½ inch thick
2 large garlic cloves, chopped fine
4 plum tomatoes
2 tbsp. chopped onion
8 fresh basil leaves

½ tsp. salt
sprinkle of black pepper
garlic powder
4 tbsp. extra virgin olive oil
¼ cup extra virgin olive oil

Preheat broiler to high (or you can grill the bread). Season ¼ cup of the olive oil with a dash of salt and garlic powder. Place bread slices on a broiler pan and brush with seasoned oil on both sides. Toast bread on each side, make sure to keep an eye on it, and be careful not to burn! Put aside.

Half and seed tomatoes, then chop and place in a small container. Pile basil leaves on top of one another and roll into a log. Thinly slice the basil and loosely combine in bowl with the tomatoes. Add 4 tbsp. of olive oil and add chopped garlic, chopped onion, salt and pepper. Gently toss the tomatoes and basil to coat. Let marinade at room temperature for at least an hour.

Place bread on a platter then spoon tomato mixture on top and serve.

CAPONATA
(Sicilian)
Serves 8

1 large eggplant (5 cups)
1 large onion, chopped (1 cup)
4 celery stalks, chopped (2 cups)
¼ cup olive oil
3 tbsp. tomato paste

3 oz. of stuffed manzanilla olives
1 oz. capers
¼ cup plus 2 tbsp. red wine vinegar
1 tbsp. sugar
¼ tsp. salt and pepper

Dice eggplant, with skin, into ½ inch pieces. Chop the olives. In a large pan over medium high flame, pour olive oil and add tomato paste, onions, eggplant, and celery, salt and pepper. Sauté for approximately 10 minutes, then add the olives (chopped) and capers, cook for another 5 minutes, then add the vinegar and the sugar.

Continue to cook for an additional 5-10 minutes until all is wilted and liquid is absorbed. Let cool and serve cold over sliced Italian bread or store in refrigerator for up to 2 weeks.

EGGPLANT PARMIGIANA
Nonna Sara's Recipe
Serves 8

2 large eggplants, sliced ¼" thick	1 tsp. salt
3 eggs	1 tsp. black pepper
2 cups parmigiano	½ cup olive oil
1 package mozzarella	½ cup vegetable oil
2 cups seasoned breadcrumbs	5 cups tomato sauce - pg. 59

Beat the eggs in a large bowl. On a large flat plate next to the egg bowl, mix the breadcrumbs, 1 cup of the Parmigiano cheese, salt and pepper. Take the eggplant slices, one by one, and dunk in egg mixture, coat all of it, then place in breadcrumbs and coat both sides. Shake off any excess breadcrumbs.

Heat ¼ cup of the olive oil with ¼ cup of the vegetable oil in a large frying pan. When oil is hot, fry the eggplant slices and cook on each side for approximately 5 minutes, turning only once, until golden color, adding more oil as needed. When all the slices are fried, put to the side until ready to assemble.

Preheat oven to 350 degrees.

Slice or grate the mozzarella. In a large 9"x12" pan, ladle some tomato sauce on bottom, then place eggplant slices, side by side, in a single layer. Then add some more tomato sauce, sprinkle with Parmigiano cheese, then the mozzarella, then add another layer of eggplant and repeat layering. Sauce, Parmigiano and mozzarella. The top layer should end with the sauce, Parmigiano and mozzarella. Cover loosely with tin foil and bake for 30 minutes, then remove foil and bake for an additional 20 minutes or until mozzarella is nice and melted.

EMPANADILLAS
(Puerto Rican)
Serves 8

1 pound of cooked protein:
    shrimp, chicken, beef or picadillo (pg. 126)
1 package empanada shells
3 tbsp. sofrito
1 tsp. adobo seasoning

2 minced garlic cloves
1 packet sazon cumino e achiote
3 tbsp. tomato sauce
2 cups vegetable oil

Chop or shred your choice of protein. Combine with sofrito, garlic, seasoning powders and tomato sauce in a bowl and let sit in refrigerator for at least an hour.

To assemble Empanadas: Empanadas are traditionally shaped like a half-moon. Take a round shell and place 1 heaping tbsp. of mixture on one side, careful not to go to the edge. Fold the other side over. To seal it, press the edges together with a fork all along the outer border, then flip it over and repeat with the fork on other side.

Lay empanadas flat on parchment paper or wax paper, side by side so they're not touching- otherwise the dough will stick.

Heat oil in deep sauté pan or deep fryer. When oil is very hot, fry a few at a time for couple of minutes on both sides, removing when they get golden-colored. Serve hot.

FIGS STUFFED WITH GORGONZOLA DRIZZLED WITH HONEY

Serves 6

18 mission figs
½ cup gorgonzola

1 ½ tbsp. extra virgin olive oil
1/3 cup fresh honey

Preheat oven to 400 degrees.

Rub each fig with olive oil then slice the figs in fourths (X shape if looking from above), stopping just before the bottom, do not slice through.

Gently open the sliced figs and carefully fill each fig with 1 tsp. gorgonzola.

Place the figs upright on a baking sheet and bake for approximately 10 minutes, until they are plump but have not burst.

Drizzle the honey on a serving platter and place figs on top, then serve.

IRIS'S POPOVERS
Serves 8

4 eggs
2 cups all-purpose flour sifted
2 cups milk

1 tsp. salt
butter

Preheat oven to 450 degrees. Generously grease cupcake pan with butter.

In a bowl, beat the eggs slightly, add the sifted flour, then milk and salt. Mix well with whisk. Pour almost 2/3 way into the cups. Place in oven for 25 minutes, then reduce heat to 350 degrees for a few more minutes until golden brown.

Let sit for 5 minutes, best when eaten while they're hot! Open the top a little bit, just enough to place a pat of butter, then close it again so butter melts.

STEAMED DUMPLINGS
Serves 8

1 lb. chopped shrimp or	1 garlic clove, finely chopped
1 lb. ground pork	2 tbsp. soy sauce
2" piece of fresh ginger, grated	1 tbsp. sesame oil
3 cups napa cabbage sliced thin	1 tbsp. wine or cooking sherry
4 scallions, sliced thin	1 egg, beaten
6 sprigs cilantro, finely chopped	1 package wonton wrappers

In a food processor or blender, combine the cabbage, scallions, cilantro, garlic and ginger. Chop fine, then place the mixture in a large bowl, add the chopped shrimp or ground pork, soy sauce, sesame oil, sherry and the egg and mix well with hands. Refrigerate for an hour before assembling the dumplings.

To Assemble Dumplings:
Using a spoon, place one heaping tbsp. of dumpling filling in the center of the wonton wrapper. Using your fingertip, wet the outer edges of the wonton wrapper with water. Fold up the sides of the dumpling into a half moon shape. Use your index finger and thumb to pinch and press the wet edges of the dough, making sure the edges are closed together. Dumplings can be cooked or frozen.

To Steam Dumplings:
Choose a wide pan and line with steam basket and 2"of water. Place a piece of parchment paper over the basket and when water comes to a boil, place the wontons next to each other, careful not to touch or dough will stick together. Place lid and steam 6-8minutes for fresh dumplings and 10 minutes for frozen.

Dipping Sauce:

2 tbsp. soy sauce	½ tbsp. rice vinegar
1 tbsp. honey	1 tsp. sesame oil

Mix all ingredients together in a small bowl. Serve with dumplings.

STUFFED MUSHROOMS WITH SAUSAGE
Serves 6

20 white mushrooms that are approximately 3 inches wide
1 pound of sausage

Preheat oven to 350 degrees.

Prepare the mushrooms, by rinsing them and removing and discarding the stems. Remove the sausage out of the casing and fill the cavity of each mushroom with the sausage. Place side by side in a baking pan. Add 3 tbsp. of water to the bottom of pan and bake for 30 minutes.

SUSHI ROLLS
Serves 6

roasted seaweed sheets
raw tuna (fresh, sashimi grade)
cucumber or avocado
sushi "sticky" rice (prepared)
4 tbsp. rice vinegar

soy sauce
pickled ginger
wasabi (prepared)
bamboo rolling mat

Prep the tuna by cutting into ½ inch thick pieces that are about 5 inches long. Cut the cucumber or avocado the same size. (If pieces are not 5 inches long it's okay to join pieces together to make the total length).

Put the sushi mat flat on your work surface with the bamboo slats arranged horizontally. Place a piece of seaweed on top. Wet your fingers in the rice vinegar bowl so rice doesn't stick to your fingers, and with your fingers, press and spread the rice in a thin coat over the seaweed. Leave a 1 inch margin on the top end without rice. Moisten this margin very slightly with your wet finger and it will serve to seal the roll like an envelope. Place tuna strips and cucumber strips horizontally on the rice 2/3 of the way down. Then carefully start to roll upward, carefully holding the filling down, roll from the front end of the mat guiding with the sushi mat toward the other end. Tighten the roll like roll cakes, pulling the mat to tighten. Remove roll from the mat and cut into 8 pieces. Serve with wasabi, soy sauce and ginger.

*Tuna can be substituted with any type of freshly caught fish.

Maria Francisco

FRIED ZUCCHINI FLOWERS
Serves 4-6

12-14 zucchini blossoms
vegetable oil
2/3 cup all-purpose flour
1 ball fresh mozzarella, optional

1 cup water
½ tsp. salt
½ tsp. garlic powder

Rinse blossoms and place on paper towel to dry.

Sift the flour through a sieve, then add salt and garlic powder.

In a large bowl, pour the water and gradually add the flour, constantly beating the mixture with a fork until all the flour has been added. The batter should have the consistency of sour cream.

Option: cut the mozzarella into strips about the size of your thumb, open the flower from the tips of the petals, and stuff the flowers with the mozzarella. Close the flower.

Pour enough oil to come ¾ inch up the sides a skillet and heat over high heat. When the oil is very hot, dip the zucchini flower in the batter and place only as many will fit in the skillet. Once a golden crust has formed on one side of the blossom, turn them over. When both sides have a nice golden crust, transfer the zucchini flowers to paper towels and season with salt and fresh cracked black pepper. Serve hot.

Maria Francisco

Chicken Broth
Chicken Soup
Chili
Cucuzza Soup (Italian Summer Squash)
Italian Wedding Soup
Lentil Soup
Meat Broth
Minestrone Soup
Mushroom Soup
New England Clam Chowder
Pasta E Fagioli
Pastina with Egg
Tuscan Farro Soup

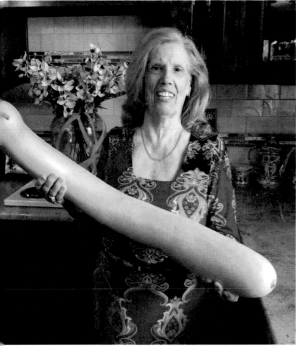

Soups

Maria Francisco

CHICKEN BROTH
Yields 2 Quarts

6 pounds chicken pieces
2 leeks, chopped
2 celery stalks, chopped
1 plum tomato quartered
1 large onion, chopped

1 large carrot, chopped
2 tbsp. minced flat leaf parsley
1 tsp. whole peppercorns
4 quarts cold water
salt to taste

Preheat oven to 400 degrees.

On a baking dish with sides, place chicken pieces (necks, backs and wings preferred) and roast for about 15 minutes or until brown, with some fat rendered out. Drain off fat, put chicken to the side.

Put leeks, celery, tomato, onion, carrot, parsley, bay leaf, and peppercorns in a large stockpot with 4 quarts of cold water. Add salt and bring to a boil. Add browned chicken pieces and return to a boil, then lower the heat and simmer gently, uncovered, for about 3 ½ hours, skimming off the scum as the broth cooks. Remove from heat and let rest for 30 minutes.

Line a colander with cheesecloth or double layer of paper towels. Strain broth and discard chicken and vegetables. Cool before refrigerating. Broth can be refrigerated for 3-4 days or frozen for up to 6 months.

CHICKEN SOUP
Serves 4

2 lbs. chicken parts
6-7 cups of water
3 chicken bouillon cubes
1 large onion quartered
3 carrots diced

2 celery stalks, halved
2 large potatoes, cubed
5 parsley springs
4 thyme sprigs
1 cup acini di pepe pasta

Make bouquet garni, French meaning bundle of herbs, by taking 6-8 sprigs of parsley, 4 sprigs of thyme, and a bay leaf and tying them together with a cooking string.

Fill a large pot with the water 2/3 way up (around 6-7 cups of water), add the chicken pieces, bouillon cubes, onion, carrots, celery, and bouquet garni and cook over medium high flame. When it comes to a boil, lower the flame to medium low and let simmer for 30 minutes. Add the potatoes and let simmer for an additional 30 minutes.

Remove the bouquet garni, the large pieces of onion and celery and the chicken pieces. Break up the chicken into chunks and discard the bones and add the chicken meat back to the pot. With a fork smash some of the potatoes and carrots to thicken the soup. Add the Acini Di Pepe pasta and cook for an additional 10 minutes or until pasta is cooked.

Serve with grated cheese.

CHILI
Serves 6

1 ½ lbs. ground beef or turkey

2 16oz. cans kidney beans

8 oz. chicken broth

1 package taco seasoning

1 can chopped chili peppers, mild

1 14 oz. can stewed tomatoes

1 bell pepper

2 onions, finely chopped

6 garlic cloves, finely chopped

1 tbsp. tabasco sauce

1 tsp. oregano

1 tsp. onion powder

1 tsp. garlic powder

Put all ingredients in a large pot. Mix well and simmer on stove for 1-2 hours. Serve with a dollop of sour cream and shredded taco cheese.

CUCUZZA pronounced Ku-KOO-za
(Italian Summer Squash Soup)

Nonna Sara Recipe
Serves 4

4 cups cucuzza, peeled and diced

¼ cup extra virgin olive oil

1 cup chopped yellow onion

2 tbsp. tomato paste

2 ½ cups water

2 potatoes, diced into 1" pieces

1 tbsp. salt

½ tsp. black pepper

3 fresh basil leaves *optional

Cucuzza is harvested in midsummer until late September.

Cut the Cucuzza in two halves, and working with one piece at a time, cut the end off and peel the skin with a potato peeler. Once peeled, cut in half, lengthwise, and if the seed are large, remove with a knife or spoon. Dice the Cucuzza into 1" pieces and set aside.

In a large 6 quart pot, pour the olive oil then add the onion, potatoes, Cucuzza pieces, salt, pepper and the tomato paste (or sauce). Stir well to coat all the pieces. Sauté on medium high heat for 5 minutes, then add the water.

Bring to a boil and simmer for about 50 minutes until Cucuzza is tender and soft. Stir occasionally. Mix in the basil leaves at the end for fresh basil taste.

Sprinkle with cheese and serve.

*Nonna Sara also made it with poached eggs (poach the egg in the soup) OR tiny bite size meatballs (prepare meatballs and add to the soup).

MARIA'S ITALIAN WEDDING CHICKEN SOUP
Serves 8

4 chicken pieces (any cut)
$^{2}/_{3}$ pound ground chicken meat
1 egg
½ cup seasoned breadcrumbs
¼ cup grated cheese
1 tsp. salt
¼ tsp. black pepper
2 carrots, diced

1 celery stalk, chopped
1 small onion, chopped
6-8 sprigs of parsley
3 sprigs of thyme
1 bay leaf
8 cups chicken stock*
1 cup of acini de pepe pasta

In a large pot, place chicken pieces, stock, carrots, celery, onion and bouquet garni (see chicken soup recipe) and cook on medium high heat. When the pot comes to a boil, lower the flame and cook on medium low flame for 30 minutes. Remove chicken pieces and discard the bones and throw the meat back into pot. Continue to cook.

In a large bowl, mix together the ground chicken, egg, breadcrumbs, grated cheese, salt and pepper. Mix well with hands then form small balls about 1 ½" big, drop them into the pot one at a time, cook for 20 minutes, add the Acini de Pepe pasta, stir and let cook for 8 minutes more. Delicious when served with a sprinkle of Parmigiano cheese.

*Instead of stock, soup can be made using bouillon.

LENTIL SOUP
Serves 4

¼ cup onion, chopped

4 tbsp. olive oil

3 tbsp. butter

¼ cup celery, finely chopped

¼ cup carrot, chopped

$^1/_3$ cup chopped pancetta

1 cup crushed tomatoes

½ pound dried lentils

6 cups meat broth (see pg. 32)

ham bone, if available

salt to taste

freshly ground black pepper

grated parmigiana cheese

Wash and drain lentils. Sort through and remove any small stones. Set aside.

In a large stockpot sauté onion in oil and butter over medium heat until a light golden brown. Add the celery and carrots and continue sautéing for 2 to 3 minutes. Add the pancetta and sauté for 1 minute. Add the tomatoes and adjust the heat so that they cook at a gentle simmer for 10 minutes, uncovered. Stir from time to time.

Add the lentils, stirring and turning them two or three times, then add the broth, ham bone if using, salt (easy on salt if you're using canned stock) and pepper. Cover and cook at a steady simmer until lentils are tender, approximately 45 minutes.

Note: Some lentils absorb more liquid than others, if this happens, add more broth or water to keep the soup from getting too thick.

MEAT BROTH
Yield 2 Quarts

2 lbs. beef or veal shinbones
1 large beef or veal knuckle bone
1 pound lean beef or veal meat
2 plum tomatoes, quartered
2 leeks, chopped
2 celery stalks, chopped
1 large onion, chopped

1 large carrot, chopped
2 tbsp. minced flat leaf parsley
1 bay leaf
1 tsp. whole peppercorns
4 quarts cold water
salt to taste

Preheat oven to 400 degrees.

Crack shinbones.

On a baking sheet with sides, roast bones and meat for about 20 minutes or until lightly browned, with some fat rendered out. Drain off the fat and set bones and meat aside.

Put tomatoes, leeks, celery, onion, carrot, parsley, bay leaf, and peppercorns in a large stockpot with 4 quarts cold water over high heat. Add salt and bring to a boil. Add browned bones and meat. Bring back to a boil, then lower heat and simmer gently, uncovered for about 3 ½ hours, skimming off the scum as the broth cooks. Remove from heat and let rest for 30 minutes.

Line a colander with cheesecloth or a double layer of paper towels. Drain broth and discard bones and vegetables. Strain broth again through a fine sieve lined with cheesecloth.

MINESTRONE SOUP
Serves 6-8

1 large onion, chopped
1 cup chopped leeks
2 cups peeled, diced potatoes
2 cups diced carrots
1 cup diced celery
1 cup diced zucchini
1 cup fresh green beans, chopped
1 can cannellini beans, drained

1 cup broccoli florets, cut in small pieces
1 tsp. thyme
¼ cup parsley, minced
4 cups water or chicken broth
2 cups san marzano tomatoes
¼ pound tubettini pasta
grated pecorino romano cheese

Heat oil in a large stockpot over medium heat. Chop tomatoes. When oil is hot, add the onion, leeks, parsley and the thyme. Sauté for about 5 minutes and then add the rest of the vegetables. Sauté for another 5 minutes, then add the water or broth and tomatoes. Add salt and pepper to taste. Bring to a boil, then simmer for about 30 minutes or until vegetables are tender. Stir occasionally, mashing the cannellini beans on the side of the pot with a spoon. Right before you turn the heat off, add the pasta and stir, let cook for 3 minutes, then turn heat off and let the minestrone cool for few minutes before eating. Serve with fresh grated cheese.

*For added flavor, I prepare a sauce on the side to pour into minestrone after its been cooked, right before serving.

Sauce: In a bowl combine 3 finely diced, plum tomatoes, 2 minced garlic cloves, ¼ cup extra virgin olive oil, ½ tsp. salt, ¼ tsp. black pepper. Mix well and store at room temperature until minestrone is done. Mix into the minestrone before serving.

MUSHROOM SOUP
Gina's Favorite
Serves 6

1 lb. white button mushrooms	3 garlic cloves, thinly sliced
1 pound shiitake mushrooms	1 ½ tsp. salt
1 oz. porcini or shiitakes, dry	¼ tsp. white pepper
½ cup olive oil	6 cups chicken stock
1 large onion, thinly sliced	1 cup heavy cream
4 sprigs of sage	2 tbsp. unsalted butter
2 sprigs rosemary	½ cup wild rice, cooked

Soak the dry mushrooms in 1 cup of warm water for 20-30 minutes, strain the soaking liquid and reserve along with the reconstituted mushrooms, until needed. Wash and thinly slice fresh mushrooms and set aside.

Cook rice in 2 cups boiling water for 20 minutes. Drain and set aside.

Heat the olive oil in a large pot over medium flame. Bundle the rosemary and sage together with a string or twine, and when the oil is hot, add the herb bundle and sizzle for a few minutes on both sides to infuse the oil. Add the onion, garlic, salt, and pepper and cook for 5 minutes, until the onion is soft and translucent. Add the white mushrooms and shiitakes.

Cook for 10 minutes, stir occasionally, the mushrooms will give off their liquid. Add the chicken stock and reconstituted mushrooms along with their soaking water. Simmer on medium low flame for 30 minutes. Remove the herbs then add the cream and butter and cook for 5 more minutes. Working in batches, puree the soup in a blender until smooth. Return to the pot and add the wild rice. Let simmer for few minutes until ready to serve.

NEW ENGLAND CLAM CHOWDER
Serves 4

4 slices bacon	2 medium potatoes, diced
1 onion, chopped	1 tsp. old bay
1 cup celery and leaves, chopped	1 cup milk
1 tsp. flour	1 cup whipping cream
2 cups of fish stock or clam juice	2 -6 ½ oz. cans of chopped clams

Fry the bacon in a large saucepan. When it's crisp, take the bacon out and put aside.

Add the onion and celery into the bacon grease and sauté until it's translucent. Stir in the flour, then pour in the fish stock and stir until it's thickened. Dump in the potatoes and seafood seasoning, bring to a boil, cover, turn down the heat and simmer for 20 minutes. Add the milk, cream, clams and clam liquid, then take it off of the fire until ready to serve.

When it's time to eat, heat through, ladle into big bowls, and crumble the bacon on top.

PASTA E FAGIOLI
Serves 6 to 8

¼ cup fine Italian olive oil

1 cup diced onion

$^1/_3$ cup diced pancetta or bacon

2 garlic cloves, peeled

2 -15 oz. cans cannellini beans

4 cups chicken broth

2 cups plum tomatoes, chopped*

¼ tsp. black pepper

1 pound tubetti

¼ cup grated parmigiano cheese

*Tomatoes can be canned or fresh. If canned, San Marzano preferred, drain before using.

In a large saucepan, combine the oil, onion, garlic and pancetta, and sauté for 5 minutes or until onions are cooked and begin to turn golden and translucent.

Stir in beans and their liquid. Add broth and pepper and bring to a boil. Add the tomatoes and return to a boil, lower heat and simmer for 20 minutes.

Meanwhile, boil salted water for pasta. When water comes to a boil, add pasta, cook for 5-8 minutes or until pasta is al dente. Drain well and add to the bean pot. Stir, let sit for a few minutes and serve with sprinkle of cheese.

PASTINA WITH EGG
(Italian Penicillin)
Serves 2

4 cups chicken stock

1 cup pastina (small star-shaped pasta)

1 egg, beaten

2 tbsp. butter

parmigiano cheese, grated

Bring 5 cups of chicken stock to a boil. Add the pastina, stir and lower the flame to a simmer. Cook as per directions on the box. Turn the gas off.

With a fork, stir in the beaten egg and add the butter. Serve with a sprinkle of cheese.

TUSCAN FARRO SOUP
Serves 4

1 can cannellini beans	1 tsp. salt
½ chopped onion	½ tsp. black pepper
1 cup diced fresh tomatoes	6 cups chicken stock
1 garlic clove, whole	1 cup farro
4 tbsp. olive oil	2 cups water

In a large pot, sauté olive oil, onion, garlic, tomatoes, salt and pepper for 5 minutes. Add the beans with their liquid and the chicken stock. Simmer for 20 minutes. Discard garlic clove.

Meanwhile, prepare the farro in a smaller saucepan. Bring farro and water to a boil. Cover with a lid and lower the flame. Simmer for 20 minutes or until the liquid is gone. Let stand for few minutes, then add the farro to the pot with the bean mixture.

Serve drizzled with truffle oil or sprinkle with cheese or both!

Arugula Salad
Caesar Salad
Caprese Salad
Coleslaw
Fennel Salad
Iceberg Wedge
Italian Potato Salad
Muffuletta
Orange Salad
Roasted Corn Salad
Seafood Salad
Seared Tuna Nicoise Salad
Tomato, Onion, and Cucumber Salad

Salads

ARUGULA SALAD

Serves 4

½ pound fresh arugula

1 medium red onion, chopped

3 large red tomatoes

¾ cup extra virgin olive oil

¼ cup balsamic vinegar

¼ tsp. sea salt

freshly ground black pepper

1 tbsp. dried oregano

Soak arugula in cold water to remove sand then drain and dry. Core and dice the tomatoes.

In a large salad bowl, prepare a tossed salad by combining the arugula with the tomatoes.

In another smaller bowl, using a whisk, blend olive oil, balsamic vinegar, sea salt, black pepper and oregano, then add the onions and mix well.

Pour the dressing over the salad and toss making sure salad is coated.

*Do not pour salad dressing over the arugula until ready to serve.

CAESAR SALAD

Serves 6

2 romaine hearts, washed and dried well

6 anchovy fillets

1 garlic clove, finely chopped

1 egg yolk

4 tbsp. fresh lemon juice

¾ tsp. dijon mustard

1 tsp. worcestershire sauce

½ cup extra virgin olive oil

½ cup grated parmigiano cheese

1 tsp. salt

fresh ground black pepper

croutons

In a large wooden bowl, using the back of a fork, crush together the anchovies, garlic and a pinch of salt to mash into a paste. Whisk in the egg yolk, fresh lemon juice, Dijon mustard and the Worchester sauce. Gradually whisk in the olive oil a little at a time, then the Parmigiano cheese. Season with salt and pepper, and add more lemon juice if desired.

Cut romaine into pieces and place on top of dressing. Toss salad when ready to serve.

Serve with shaved parmigiano and croutons.

CAPRESE SALAD
Serves 4

1 pound fresh mozzarella
4 large heirloom tomatoes
½ cup fresh basil leaves, torn
sea salt

freshly cracked black pepper
balsamic vinegar
extra virgin olive oil

Slice the fresh mozzarella and the heirloom tomatoes each ¼ inch thick. Arrange on a serving platter (fresh mozzarella, tomato, mozzarella, tomato etc.). Sprinkle with fresh basil, salt and pepper. Drizzle with equal parts olive oil and balsamic vinegar.

COLESLAW
Serves 8

1 package of coleslaw mix
¼ onion, finely chopped
¼ cup sugar
1 tsp. salt
¼ tsp. black pepper
¼ cup milk

¼ cup butter milk
½ cup mayonnaise
1 ½ tbsp. vinegar
2 ½ tbsp. lemon juice
1 tsp. mustard seed

In a large bowl, combine the mayonnaise, butter milk, milk, sugar, salt, pepper, vinegar, lemon juice and mustard seed. Mix well then add the coleslaw mix and onion. Toss well and refrigerate for at least 2 hours before serving.

FINOCCHIO (FENNEL) SALAD
Serves 6

1 fennel bulb

½ onion

2 plum tomatoes

15 pimento stuffed green olives

3 tbsp. capers

6 anchovies

juice of ½ lemon

$1/8$ cup extra virgin olive oil

salt and black pepper to taste

Slice fennel thinly into 2-3 inch long pieces. Chop onion finely. Core and chop tomatoes. Slice olives in half. Cut anchovies into small pieces.

Place all ingredients in a large bowl and toss well. Add salt and pepper to taste.

ICEBERG WEDGE WITH
BLUE CHEESE AND BACON DRESSING

Serves 4

1 whole iceberg lettuce

1 cup grape tomatoes

1 garlic clove, finely chopped

½ cup sour cream

1 cup mayonnaise

2 tbsp. fresh lemon juice

1 tsp. fresh ground black pepper

1 cup crumbled blue cheese

1 tsp. salt

½ pound thick cut bacon

Core and cut iceberg lettuce in 4 wedges. Cut tomatoes in half.

In a bowl, mix the sour cream, mayonnaise and the lemon juice, salt and pepper. Then add the blue cheese and stir until well blended. Cover and chill.

Cut bacon into 2 inch pieces and cook in a skillet until golden brown and beginning to crisp.

Arrange salad wedges on a plate, scatter grape tomatoes over and around the lettuce, and pour dressing on the lettuce and top with bacon pieces.

ITALIAN POTATO SALAD
Nonna Sara's Recipe
Serves 8

6 large potatoes, peeled
¼ onion, finely chopped
²/₃ cup olive oil
½ cup wine vinegar

¼ cup chopped fresh parsley
1 tsp. black pepper
2 tsp. salt

Bring a large pot of salted water to a boil and add the potatoes whole, cook until tender but firm, about 20 minutes. Make sure you don't overcook. Drain, cool and chop into pieces.

In a large bowl, mix together the olive oil, vinegar, salt, pepper and parsley. Add the potatoes and toss to evenly coat. Let sit at room temperature or in fridge until ready to serve.

MUFFULETTA
(New Orleans Sandwich Mix)
Paul's Recipe

15 oz. green stuffed olives

15 oz. black pitted olives

3.5 oz. capers, drained

2 garlic cloves

5 sprigs parsley

1 celery stalk

3 anchovies (optional)

¼ cup extra virgin olive oil

1 tbsp. red wine vinegar

1 tbsp. lemon juice

½ tsp. cracked pepper

1 tsp. salt

1 tbsp. dried oregano

Finely chop the green olives, black olives, capers, garlic, parsley, anchovies and the celery and place in a large bowl. Add the olive oil, wine vinegar, lemon juice, salt, pepper, and oregano. Mix well and let sit at room temperature for at least 2 hours, stirring often. Store in refrigerator for up to 6 months.

Spread generously over Italian bread and layer the sandwich with mortadella, salami, ham, capicola and provolone cheese.

ORANGE SALAD
(Sicilian Recipe)
Nonna Sara Recipe
Serves 4

3 navel or blood oranges
¼ cup olive oil
2 tbsp. water

½ tsp. sea salt
¼ tsp. fresh ground black pepper
pinch of oregano

Peel the oranges, then separate the segments. Peel the skins, remove the seeds and cut in half. Place in bowl and add oil, salt, pepper, and oregano. Toss together to coat.

ROASTED CORN SALAD
(New Orleans)
Serves 12

12 ears of corn, husk peeled off
¼ cup olive oil
1 ½ cups mayonnaise
¼ cup sour cream
3 garlic cloves, minced
2 tsp. salt

½ tsp. black pepper
1 tsp. cayenne
juice of 1 and ½ limes
1 tsp. cilantro
¼ cup grated parmigiano cheese
½ tsp. hot pepper

Place corn on a baking sheet and brush them all over with olive oil, sprinkle with a little salt. You can either grill or bake in the oven at 350 degrees until golden, about 20-30 minutes. When cooked, let sit for a few minutes to cool off.

Make the dressing: In a bowl, combine the mayonnaise, sour cream, then add the garlic, black pepper, salt, cayenne, cilantro and lime juice, then stir in the grated cheese, mix well and refrigerate.

Using a knife, remove the kernels from the corn husks and place in a large bowl. Add $^2/_3$ of the dressing, mix well (add a little more of the dressing if you think it needs more). Refrigerate until ready to serve.

Maria Francisco

COLD SEAFOOD SALAD
(Frutte di Mare)
Serves 8

1 pound fresh, small squid

1 pound shrimp

1 cup jumbo lump crabmeat

½ cup fine extra virgin olive oil

¼ cup fresh lemon juice

2 tsp. salt

½ tsp. black pepper

2 garlic cloves, minced

2 celery stalks and leaves, chopped fine

½ cup chopped flat leaf parsley

6 lemon wedges, for garnish

10 green olives with pimentos

Rinse squid under cold water, separate the bodies from the tentacles. Remove backbone. Peel and devein shrimp.

Place about a quart of water in a medium pot. When water comes to a boil, add the squid and 1 tbsp. salt. Bring pot to a rolling boil. Lower heat to a gentle boil and cook for about 5 minutes or until squid are very tender. Overcooking the squid will make them rubbery. Remove from heat and run cold water into the pot until water is cool. Drain, pat dry and cut the body into small ringlets and cut the tentacles in half. Place to side and cover with a damp paper towel.

Place about 2 inches water in a pot with ½ tsp. salt and bring to a boil. Add the shrimp, cover and let steam for few minutes until shrimp are no longer translucent. Remove from heat, drain and let cool.

In a large bowl, whisk together the olive oil, lemon juice, garlic, and 2 tsp. salt and ½ tsp. pepper to taste, adjust salt if needed. Add the calamari, the shrimp, olives, celery, and parsley. Toss well to coat. Cover with plastic wrap and refrigerate for about 30 minutes or until ready to serve. Add the crabmeat and toss gently to coat, then serve garnished with lemon wedges.

SEARED TUNA NICOISE SALAD
Gina's Favorite
Serves 4

3 large eggs

1 cup green beans

4 small red potatoes

2 – 6oz. tuna steaks

¼ cup olive oil

1 tsp. dijon mustard

1/8 cup red wine vinegar

2/3 cup grape tomatoes, halved

¼ cup pitted nicoise olives

1 boston lettuce or bibb lettuce

salt and pepper to taste

Hard boil the egg and let cool 15 minutes. Peel and cut each egg into 4 slices, put aside.

Place potatoes in pan, cover with water and cook for minutes or until potatoes are tender. Drain and put aside to cool, then slice each into 4 slices. In the same pot, bring 3" salted water to a boil, then add green beans. Cook for 3 minutes, then drain and plunge beans into ice water for 1 minute, drain well.

Heat a large cast iron skillet or frying pan on medium high heat. Coat pan with a little oil. Sprinkle tuna steaks with some salt and pepper on both sides. When pan is hot, add tuna and sear for 2 minutes on each side, or until desired degree of doneness. Let cool and slice thinly across the grain.

Combine the olive oil, vinegar, mustard, salt and pepper with a whisk. Add the tomatoes and chopped olives and toss.

On a large serving platter, place torn lettuce, then green beans, egg slices, potatoes, tuna slices, then top with the tomato mixture. Divide salad onto 4 plates.

TOMATO, RED ONION, CUCUMBER AND BASIL SUMMER SALAD

Serves 6

8 very ripe tomatoes

1 cucumber

1 cup extra virgin olive oil

1 large red onion

3 tbsp. red wine vinegar

8 fresh basil leaves, torn

1 tsp. dried oregano

½ tsp. salt to taste

fresh ground black pepper

Wash and core tomatoes. Cut into 8 wedges each. Cut cucumber in half lengthwise, scrape out seeds with a spoon and dice. Slice red onion thinly.

In a bowl, add all ingredients and toss well to combine. Adjust salt, (add some more if needed). Best if let to marinate in the refrigerator for 30 minutes before eating.

Sunday Sauce
Tomato Sauce
Bolognese Meat Sauce
Aglione Sauce
Pesto Sauce
Tomato Sauce for Canning

Homemade Pasta
Homemade Pici Pasta

Creamy Pesto Farfalle Pasta
Filetto Di Pomodoro Pasta
Pasta with Sausage, Mushrooms and Asparagus
Lasagna
Linguine Aglio E Olio
Linguine with White Clam Sauce
Manicotti
Orecchiette with Broccoli Rabe and Sausage
Pasta Alla Carbonara
Pasta Alla Puttanesca
Pasta Cacio E Pepe
Pasta Al Forno with Cauliflower
Pasta with Pisellini
Pasta with Salsa Cruda
Pastelon – Puerto Rican Lasagna
Patten Ave Crab Sauce with Angel Hair
Shells with Ricotta
Ricotta Cheese
Risotto Porcini

Pasta and Sauces

SUNDAY SAUCE

Serves 8

1 pound beef short ribs	6 oz. can tomato paste
1 pound pork neck bones*	3 28 oz. cans plum tomatoes**
1 pound Italian sausages	1 tbsp. salt
½ cup good Italian olive oil	1 tsp. black pepper
4 garlic cloves, finely chopped	meatballs, pg. 111
½ onion, chopped	

*Neck bones can be replaced with 1 lb. pork loin cut into 2 inch pieces.

**Hand crushed, San Marzano Italian plum tomatoes preferred.

Heat the oil in a large saucepan, big enough to hold all the meat. Add garlic and onion and sauté for a couple of minutes, then add the meat pieces, turning them to brown on all sides. As meat is browned, remove from pan and set aside.

Stir the tomato paste into ¼ cup water and stir the mixture in the oil. Cook, stirring constantly for 2 minutes. Stir in the 3 cans of tomatoes, raise heat and bring to a boil. Add 1 cup of cold water, then return beef and pork to the sauce and add salt and pepper. Bring to boil and let boil 5 minutes.

Lower the heat and partially cover the pan. Let simmer for about an hour, stirring occasionally to make sure nothing sticks to the bottom. If sauce becomes too thick, add ¼ cup water at a time. After meat has been cooking for an hour, add meatballs and sausage. Cook for another hour, remember to stir occasionally.

Remove meat from the sauce and serve sauce over pasta. Eat meat as a separate course.

TOMATO SAUCE
Serves 8

2 – 28 oz. cans plum tomatoes*
¼ cup italian olive oil
2 garlic cloves, finely chopped
¼ onion, finely chopped

4 fresh basil leaves
2 tsp. salt
½ tsp. black pepper

*Hand crushed San Marzano preferred.

Heat olive oil in a large pot over medium low flame, add the garlic and the onion and sauté for a couple of minutes, careful not to burn the garlic, then add the crushed tomatoes, salt and pepper. Stir well and raise flame to medium high and cook for a few minutes, until comes to a boil. Lower the flame a bit to medium, add basil leaves and continue cooking for 20-25 minutes, stirring occasionally.

BOLOGNESE MEAT SAUCE
Serves 6

¼ cup olive oil	1 cup milk
1 ½ lbs. ground beef/veal mix	½ cup heavy cream
28 oz. can crushed tomatoes	3 garlic cloves, finely chopped
¼ lb. pancetta or bacon, diced	¼ tsp. nutmeg, freshly ground
1 small onion, chopped	2 tsp. salt
2 carrots, finely chopped	1 tsp. black pepper
1 cup red wine	

In a large pot, sauté garlic and onion in olive oil on medium flame for a few minutes, until translucent. Add pancetta and cook for 5 minutes until pancetta gets crispy. Add the carrots, sauté 5 more minutes, then add the meat. Sauté until meat is browned. Turn up flame to high and add the wine. Cook for a few minutes until the alcohol evaporates. Add the milk and cook until thickened. Add the tomatoes, San Marzano preferred, season with salt, pepper and nutmeg. Lower the flame and let simmer for 1 hour.

At the end of the hour, add the heavy cream and cook for 5 more minutes.

Prepare Pasta:
Boil water and 2 tbsp. salt. When water comes to a boil add 1 pound pasta. Stir and cook as per instructions on the box, or until al dente. Drain well and add the Bolognese sauce and mix. Top with grated cheese.

Delicious when served with pappardelle pasta.

AGLIONE SAUCE
For 1 Pound of Pasta

4 cups peeled, diced plum tomatoes (fresh if possible)
6 large garlic cloves
1/3 cup extra virgin olive oil

1 tsp. salt
1 tsp. pepper
pinch crushed red pepper

Pour oil into a large sauté pan over medium heat, when the oil is hot, add the garlic cloves. Sauté for 2-3 minutes until the garlic turns lightly golden brown. Do not burn. Add the tomatoes, salt and pepper.

Cook the sauce for 20 minutes until the tomatoes melt and sauce thickens. Add the crushed red pepper and adjust salt if needed. Remove the garlic pieces and press through a food mill (or squash with a fork) and add them back to the sauce. Sauté for an additional 5 minutes.

Serve over homemade Pici Pasta, pg 65.

BASIC BASIL PESTO RECIPE
Yields: 1 cup

3 garlic cloves

1/3 cup pignoli nuts

2 cups fresh basil leaves

½ cup extra virgin olive oil

½ cup grated parmigiano cheese

1 tsp. salt

½ tsp. black pepper

½ tsp. red pepper flakes, optional

Lightly brown the pignoli nuts over medium heat in a frying pan. In the blender, add and pulse the garlic cloves and pignoli nuts, then add the olive oil, basil leaves, salt, pepper and pepper flakes. Blend for about 1 minute, then scrape down the sides and add the grated cheese. Blend until mixture becomes creamy and there are no lumps. Store in refrigerator or freezer.

*When making pasta with pesto: Cook the pasta, drain, then pour pasta back in pot and add ½ cup of pesto to a pound of cooked pasta, or more, if you like. Mix well and serve warm.

TOMATO SAUCE FOR CANNING

Yields approximately 14 - 1 quart mason jars

1 bushel of plum tomatoes (35-40 pounds) preferably "San Marzano"
30 fresh basil leaves, rinsed and totally dried   4 tbsp. salt

Sterilize your jars and lids in the dishwasher on the sterilize cycle or by hand. To sterilize by hand, wash each jar with soap and water. Fill your canner or large pot with enough water to cover the jars by at least 1 inch and bring to a simmer. Using tongs, tilt the jars so they fill with the hot water. Pour the water out and drain upside down on paper towels until completely dry. Repeat with the lids. When jars are dry, stack the jars in the oven on their sides with opening facing you. Bake at 175 degrees until you are ready to fill with hot sauce.

Fill a large stock pot less than halfway with water and bring to a boil. Add tomatoes a few at a time, don't overflow the water. After water returns to a boil and the skins are cracked, cook 10 more minutes. Drain the tomatoes in colanders for 5 minutes. Repeat until all the tomatoes are cooked and drained.

The goal of this step is to separate the tomato pulp from the undesired skins and seeds. Break up drained tomatoes by pulsing in a blender for a few seconds, then run the mixture through a tomato strainer "passatutto" fitted with the largest-hole disk. Discard the skins and seeds. *If you are using an automatic electric tomato strainer, skip the blender step.

In a very large pot, add the tomato pulp and salt. Split the salt if using two pots. Bring sauce to a rolling boil, stirring often, then lower the flame and simmer on low for 10 minutes. Carefully remove the warm jars from the oven using mitts or tongs. Put 2 basil leaves in the bottom of each jar, then ladle in the simmering sauce and put the lids on, tightly screwing on the rings. Place the jars next to one another on a flat surface, such as on the floor out of the way, then cover with a towel to keep them warm. The heat will invert the lids and form the seal. Do not move or disturb for 48 hours.

*Jars may be stored in a cupboard or in a basement for 2-3 years, as the sauce preserved in a sterile environment. If the lid is not inverted after 48 hours, do not store. You may refrigerate and use the jar for up to 1 week.

Maria Francisco

HOMEMADE PASTA RECIPE
Nonna Sara Recipe
Serves 4

3¾ cups semolina flour   pinch of salt
4 eggs

Place the flour on a clean smooth surface, create a well in the middle of the flour and add the salt and eggs. Using a fork, whisk the eggs together and while whisking, slowly begin to incorporate the flour a little at a time until the mixture becomes creamy and eventually becomes too thick to continue whisking. With floured hands, finish combining the flour until the dough no longer sticks to your hands. Knead on a floured surface for about 5 minutes, or until it becomes smooth, elastic and a finger poked into the surface of the dough bounces back.

Divide the rested pasta dough into four pieces, and, keeping the pieces that are not in use, covered. Roll out the pasta into thin sheets with a rolling pin to about 1/8 inch thick. Let the pasta sheet "dry" for a few minutes before rolling it into a long log. Dust the area with plenty of flour so doesn't stick. Then with a sharp knife, cut ¼ inch strips and when the whole log has been cut, unroll each pasta piece and hang on a broom stick or transfer to a floured plate or board. Let pasta harden for at least an hour before cooking.

In a large sauce pan, bring water and salt and 2 tbsp. of oil to a boil. Then add the fresh pasta and cook for only few minutes, until pasta floats to the top. Strain pasta and immediately add little bit of olive oil, so pasta doesn't stick, then add your sauce.

*Fresh pasta will absorb most of the sauce so put extra sauce on the side. When pasta is plated, top each plate with the extra sauce before serving. This pasta is best served with a cream based sauce such as carbonara.

HOMEMADE PICI PASTA
Serves 4

3-4 cups double 00 flour   1 egg
1 cup warm water add ½ tsp. salt   3 cups cornmeal for dusting

*Can substitute 3-4 cups Double 00 flour for 1 ½ - 2 cups semolina flour + 1 ½ – 2 cups all-purpose flour.

On a wooden cutting board (preferred), combine the flour and form a well in the center. Add the egg, and beat with a fork. Pour the water into the well a little at a time and, using a fork, start scraping some of the flour from inner sides of the well into the water. Slowly add more water and incorporate more and more of the flour. When it becomes a shaggy mess, it's time to use your hands to knead it.

Dust the surface with flour so dough doesn't stick. Knead for 8-10 minutes until dough is smooth, add more flour as needed. You want a nice soft flour, not sticky. Form into a ball, cover with plastic wrap and let rest for 30 minutes.

Meanwhile place cornmeal in a large bowl and put aside for dusting.

Dust your work area with flour, and cut your dough into 4 pieces. Working with 1 piece of dough at a time, flatten first with your hands, then flour both sides and flatten with a rolling pin until dough is about 1/8" thick. Cut into 1/2"strips and with your palms flat, roll each strip from the center outwards rapidly. The skinnier, the better. Lengths will be irregular, but should be no longer than 8". Place each piece in the cornmeal bowl and coat well. Then shake off most of the cornmeal and place pasta flat on a dry surface. Bring a large pot of salted water to a boil, add pici and cook for 3 minutes until pasta floats to top. Drain well and combine with Aglione Sauce (recipe below) or your favorite sauce. Pici pasta is to be eaten within a couple hours of preparation.

CREAMY PESTO FARFALLE PASTA

Serves 6-8 people

1 cup pesto, pg. 62
¼ cup heavy cream
3 tbsp. olive oil

16 oz. farfalle (bowtie) pasta
1 tsp. salt to taste
fresh cracked black pepper

In a large sauté pan, heat oil over medium heat. Add the pesto and mix into the oil. Be sure to stir often as the pesto warms. When pesto is warmed and just a little bubbly, slowly incorporate the heavy cream with a whisk. If you want to add a little more cream, go for it!

Turn down the heat and continue to stir the cream and the pesto. Add salt and pepper to taste. Set aside.

Meanwhile, in a large saucepan, bring salted water to a boil. Add the farfalle "butterfly" pasta, stir well and cook until "al dente" approximately 8 minutes or so.

Drain pasta, then add to the pesto sauce, tossing to cover all of the pasta. Serve warm. Add grated parmigiano cheese if you like.

FILETTO DI POMODORO PASTA

Serves 4

6 cups plum tomatoes

$^1/_3$ cup extra virgin olive oil

4 oz. chopped pancetta or bacon

¾ cup chopped onion

8 fresh basil leaves, chopped

Salt and pepper to taste

1 pound fusilli pasta

pecorino romano, grated

Crush plum tomatoes, preferably San Marzano, by hand.

Heat olive oil in a large sauté pan over medium heat. When the oil is hot, add onion and pancetta and sauté for about 5 minutes until the pancetta is slightly crisp.

Stir in the tomatoes and bring to a low boil. Lower the heat and simmer for approximately 30 minutes, stirring occasionally, until the tomatoes have cooked down somewhat. Remove tomato skins. Add salt and the fresh basil leaves and pepper. Stir well and put aside.

Cook the fusilli in rapidly boiling salted water until cooked al dente. Drain, then return drained pasta to the pot. Add a cup of tomato sauce, mix well, then pour Fusilli into a pasta bowl. Spoon the remaining sauce over the top. Serve with grated cheese.

PASTA WITH SAUSAGE, MUSHROOMS AND ASPARAGUS IN CREAM SAUCE

Gabe's Recipe

Serves 8

8 sausage links

16 oz. portabella mushrooms

10 asparagus spears

2 medium onions, chopped

2 garlic cloves, chopped

16 oz. tomato sauce

½ stick butter

¼ cup olive oil

1 cup of heavy cream

½ cup grated pecorino cheese

½ cup grated parmigiano cheese

2 bay leaves

1 tsp. ground nutmeg

1 chicken bouillon cube

2 large eggs, beaten

2 lbs. rigatoni pasta

Take the sausage out of casings and cut into 1 inch pieces. Slice mushrooms. Cut ends off of asparagus and discard, and slice asparagus into ½ inch pieces. Set aside.

In a large pan, melt butter and olive oil. Sauté garlic and onion for 5 minutes. Turn the gas to medium high, add the mushrooms and cook for 5 minutes until mushrooms shrink somewhat. Add the sausage pieces, stirring until sausage is partially cooked, then add the asparagus, sauté 5 minutes. Add tomato sauce, bay leaves, nutmeg, and bullion. Cook on low for 10 minutes. Turn gas off, then add the heavy cream, pecorino and parmigiano cheeses. Stir well, put aside.

Meanwhile, boil water with a little salt for pasta. When water comes to boil, add rigatoni. Continue cooking until pasta is done. Drain pasta, put back in the pot, and add the 2 beaten eggs. Stir quickly, then add the meat and mushroom mixture, continue to stir. Add more cheese if you like. Serve hot.

LASAGNA
Serves 10

2 lbs. lean ground beef	½ tsp. pepper
1 lb. sweet italian sausage	2 lbs. ricotta cheese
1 cup onion, chopped	2 cups grated mozzarella
2 cloves garlic, minced	1 egg, beaten
3 28 oz. cans crushed tomatoes	1 cup pecorino cheese , grated
3 tbsp. tomato paste	1 lb. fresh mozzarella sliced
1 cup water	¼ cup olive oil
1 tsp. salt	1 lb. lasagna noodles

Preheat oven to 350 degrees

In a large saucepan, heat the oil over medium high heat. Add the onion and garlic and sauté for 2-3 minutes then add the ground beef and the sausage (out of the casings). Sauté until the meat is browned, stirring and breaking up the meat pieces. If the meat is fatty, discard some of the fat liquid with a spoon. Stir in the tomato paste, tomatoes and water. Add salt and pepper. Simmer for about 45 minutes, or until sauce gets thick. Set aside.

In a large bowl combine the ricotta cheese, egg, ½ cup grated mozzarella and ½ cup grated pecorino cheese.

Meanwhile, in a large pot of boiling water, cook the lasagna noodles halfway. Drain well in a colander and then run under cold water to stop the cooking process. Place noodles on top of damp kitchen towels and cover with damp towels until ready to use.

Ladle a thin layer of meat sauce into a lasagna pan. Cover with some of the noodles, laid lengthwise. Layer with meat sauce and then some of the ricotta cheese, the grated mozzarella cheese and then the pecorino cheese. Continue layering the pasta, sauce and cheeses. Finish with a layer of meat sauce and cover with slices of mozzarella cheese. Bake for 45 minutes or until mozzarella has melted and lasagna is bubbling. Let cool for 15 minutes before serving.

LINGUINE AGLIO E OLIO
(Garlic and Oil)
Serves 4

1 pound linguine

½ cup extra virgin olive oil

4 whole garlic cloves, crushed

3 large garlic cloves, minced

salt and pepper to taste

2 tbsp. chopped parsley

pecorino romano, grated

Cook linguine in a large pot of rapidly boiling salted water until al dente.

While linguine is cooking, heat oil in medium sauté pan and add the 4 whole, crushed garlic cloves. Cook for 2 minutes then discard the garlic cloves. Add the minced garlic and cook for couple of more minutes or until garlic is golden, add salt and pepper. Be careful not to burn the garlic. Remove from heat and keep warm.

Drain linguine, reserving ½ cup of the pasta water. Return drained pasta and the reserved pasta water to the pot and add the oil mixture. Toss well, serve in pasta dishes and sprinkle with parsley and grated cheese.

LINGUINE WITH WHITE CLAM SAUCE
Serves 6

3 dozen cherrystone clams
2 garlic cloves, finely chopped
½ cup olive oil
1 cup clam broth or juice

¼ cup dry white wine
1 pound linguine pasta
10 sprigs parsley chopped

*Make sure clams are fresh and shut closed when you purchase them. Discard any open clams. Can alternatively use 1 dozen cherrystone clams plus 2- 6 ½ oz. cans of chopped clams

Soak the clams in cold water for 10 minutes, this will release any sand they have. Scrub the shells, then rinse them under cold water.

If using all fresh clams, place 2 dozen clams in large pot with ¼ cup water. Cover with tight lid and bring to a boil, simmer until all shells open. Remove clams, saving 1 cup of broth. Remove one dozen of the clams from their shells and chop, leaving the other dozen whole in their opened shells.

In the same saucepan, sauté garlic in the olive oil, when garlic begins to turn golden, add the 1 dozen whole clams in their shells, along with the 1 cup of broth (or 1 cup of clam juice) and the white wine. Cover and continue cooking until alcohol from wine is burned off, about 5-10 min.

Meanwhile, cook the linguine in a large, deep pot in rapidly boiling salted water until al dente (hard to the bite). Drain linguine.

Uncover the saucepan and add 1 dozen chopped fresh clams, or canned chopped clams (if using canned), and parsley. Cook for 1 minute.

Return drained linguine to large pot, and over medium heat, stir in the clam sauce. Using a wooden spoon, toss together. Remove from heat and serve.

MANICOTTI (CANNELLONI) HOMEMADE
Nonna Sara's Recipe
Serves 6

Cannelloni shells:

6 eggs

2 cups flour (semolina preferred)

2 cups water

¼ tsp. salt

*Use a small 6 inch non-stick frying pan for best results, wiped with an oiled paper towel.

Beat the eggs, flour, water and salt with hand mixer, until mixture is smooth.

Heat a non-stick frying pan, then pour ¼ cup of batter, tipping the pan immediately after pouring to get the batter evenly over the bottom of the pan, forming perfect thin circles like a crepe. After about 15 seconds, turn it over for another 15 seconds, then take them out and place on a plate.

Ricotta Filling:

3 ½ cups ricotta cheese, pg. 81

2 cups mozzarella, shredded

½ cup grated parmigiano cheese

2 eggs, beaten

½ tsp. salt

¼ tsp. ground black pepper

35oz. tomato sauce, pg 59

Preheat oven to 350 degrees. Place all stuffing ingredients in a large bowl and mix well.

Cover the bottom of a 13x9 baking pan with sauce.

Take a round pasta shell and in the center place about 2 tbsp. ricotta mix. Fold the sides in first, then fold the top over the bottom part, place overlapping side down in the pan, next to each other. Pour the remainder of the sauce over filled pasta, sprinkle with cheese and mozzarella. Then cover with foil and bake for 35 minutes or until hot and bubbly.

ORECCHIETE WITH BROCCOLI RABE AND SAUSAGE

Serves 6

¼ cup extra virgin olive oil

4 garlic cloves, chopped fine

1 pound Italian sausage

1 lb. broccoli rabe cooked pg.146

1 cup broccoli rabe water

1 chicken bouillon cube or

1 tsp. salt

1 pound orecchiette pasta

1 cup grated pecorino romano

Heat oil in sauté pan. Add garlic and sauté over medium heat for couple of minutes. Chop sausage and add to the pan and cook until meat is cooked. Add cooked broccoli rabe to the sausage along with the broccoli rabe water and the chicken bouillon cube. Raise heat and cook until sauce is hot.

Meanwhile, cook orecchiette in rapidly boiling salted water until done.

Drain orecchiette, return to the pot and place over medium heat and stir in ¾ cup of the broccoli rabe and sausage mixture. Toss together for a minute, then remove from heat and pour into a pasta platter. Spoon the remainder broccoli rabe sauce over the pasta and sprinkle with grated cheese. Serve immediately.

PASTA ALLA CARBONARA
Serves 6

1 medium onion, finely chopped
6 parsley stems, finely chopped
¼ cup extra virgin olive oil
4 tbsp. butter
8 oz. pancetta or bacon

½ cup heavy cream
8 oz. grated parmigiano cheese
2 eggs
1 lb. spaghetti

In a sauté pan, on medium low flame, heat the olive oil and butter. When butter has melted, add the onions, sauté couple of minutes, then add chopped pancetta and cook for few minutes until pancetta is crisp. Set aside.

In a bowl, whisk the eggs, cream and cheese, and set aside.

Use a large pot and fill ¾ way with water and 2 tbsp. of salt. When water comes to a boil, add the spaghetti and cook until al dente, approximately 6 minutes. Drain the pasta and return to the pot. Add the onion and pancetta mixture and stir over high heat until pasta is coated. Remove the pasta from the heat and add the egg, cheese and cream mixture. Toss until pasta is coated. Season with fresh ground pepper and sprinkle with parsley and serve immediately.

PASTA ALLA PUTTANESCA

Serves 4

1 pound pasta
¼ cup virgin olive oil
1 cup finely chopped onion
6 anchovy fillets, chopped
3 garlic cloves, finely chopped
4 cups crushed tomatoes

¼ cup white wine
1 cup pitted, black olives, preferably
   brine cured
2 tbsp. capers
salt and pepper to taste

In a large sauté pan, add the oil, onion and garlic and sauté over medium-low heat for about 5 minutes. Stir in the anchovies until they dissolve into the oil. Raise the heat and add the wine. Bring to a boil and stir in the tomatoes with their juices, olives, capers and return to a boil. Lower the heat and simmer for 5 minutes. Taste and adjust seasoning with salt and pepper and simmer for 10 more minutes.

Meanwhile, cook the pasta in a large pot in rapidly boiling salted water until al dente.

Drain pasta, return to pot and mix with half of the sauce. Pour into a serving platter and spoon remaining sauce over the top.

PASTA CACIO E PEPE

Serves 4

¼ cup ground black pepper

½ cup olive oil

6 tbsp. unsalted butter

¼ cup grated parmigiano cheese

¼ cup grated pecorino cheese

salt to taste

1 lb. linguini pasta

*Use course ground pepper. Best if you use freshly ground peppercorns.

Bring a large pot of generously salted water to a boil and cook pasta until al dente. During the last minute of cooking, remove 1 ½ cups pasta cooking water and reserve.

In a skillet or large pan, heat the black pepper and toast, stirring for about 15 seconds. Add the oil and butter until melted. Add ½ cup of the pasta cooking water, keep on low flame.

Drain pasta and immediately add to skillet, stirring for 2 minutes. Add the remaining pasta water as needed so pasta doesn't stick. Turn off heat, let rest for a minute, then add cheeses, stirring and shaking the pan until a sauce forms. Drizzle a little bit of good olive oil on top and garnish with more cheese if desired.

PASTA AL FORNO WITH CAULIFLOWER
(Sicilian Style)
Nonna Sara's Recipe
Serves 8

1 large cauliflower, cut into small pieces

4 scallions, chopped

1 lb. sausage (out of casing)

1 cup tomato sauce

$^1/_3$ cup olive oil

8 oz. shredded mozzarella

1 cup grated parmigiano cheese

salt and pepper to taste

1 pound rigatoni pasta

Preheat oven to 350 degrees

Fill a large pot half way with water and 2 tbsp. of salt. When water comes to boil, add the cauliflower and cook for 15 minutes on medium flame. Drain cauliflower and put aside.

In a large sauté pan, add the olive oil and scallions and sauté for few minutes until scallions are wilted. Add the cauliflower to the pan, salt and pepper and mix well. Cook for 3 minutes, then put the mixture aside. In the same pan, cook the sausage, stirring and breaking it up. When sausage is cooked, drain the fat, then add the sausage to the cauliflower mixture.

In a large pot, cook the pasta. Bring salted water to a boil and add the rigatoni. Cook for 8 minutes or until pasta is half-way cooked, then drain the pasta and put back in the pot. Add the tomato sauce, cauliflower, sausage mixture, mozzarella and the Parmigiano cheese. Place in baking pan, cover with tin foil, and bake for 45 minutes.

PASTA WITH PISELLINI
Nonna Sara's Recipe
Paul's Favorite
Serves 4

1 ½ cups frozen peas
4 tbsp. chopped onion
3 tbsp. tomato paste
½ cup olive oil
1 tbsp. salt

½ tsp. black pepper
12 oz. ditalini pasta
6 cups water
parmigiano cheese, grated

In a large pot, over medium high heat, pour the olive oil, add the peas, onion and tomato paste, salt and pepper. Sauté for about 3-5 minutes then add the water. Raise the heat and let come to a boil, then lower the flame to medium low and cook for about 20-25 minutes.

Taste and adjust the salt, when the peas are cooked, add the pasta and continue cooking for 8-10 minutes or until pasta is done. Let it sit for few minutes before serving. Serve with grated Parmigiano cheese.

PASTA WITH SALSA CRUDA
(Italian Summer Sauce with Raw Tomatoes)
Serves 4-6

6 ripe plum tomatoes
10 basil leaves, chopped
2 garlic cloves, chopped fine
1/3 cup extra virgin olive oil

1 pound pasta
1 tsp. salt
fresh cracked black pepper
parmigiano cheese, grated

Seed the tomatoes and chop them fine. In a large pasta serving bowl, mix together the tomatoes, basil, garlic and olive oil. Add salt and pepper. Stir and lightly press the ingredients with a wooden spoon to incorporate flavors. Let sit at room temperature at least 30 minutes or up to a day.

Just before serving, cook the pasta in salted water. Drain the pasta and while steaming hot, place the pasta on top of the tomato sauce. Let it sit for a minute before tossing the pasta. Top with grated parmigiano cheese.

PASTELON
(Puerto Rican Lasagna)
Serves 6

1 medium spanish onion	2 cups shredded sharp cheddar
1 green pepper	2 tsp. dried oregano
½ cup olives w/pimentos	2 tsp. adobo seasoning
2 garlic cloves	2 tbsp. apple cider vinegar
4 ripe sweet plantains	1 can (15 oz.) tomato sauce
1 lb. ground beef	¼ cup vegetable oil
2 cups shredded mozzarella	2 eggs beaten

Chop onion, garlic and peppers. Slice plantains into thin long slices. Cut olives in half.

Heat oven to 350 degrees. In a large pan, add 2 tbsp. of oil and sauté onions, peppers, garlic for 2 minutes. Add meat, oregano, Adobo and vinegar, cook until browned. Add olives and tomato sauce. Reduce heat and simmer 5 minutes. Put aside.

In a large frying pan, heat ¼ cup oil over medium heat. When hot, add several plantain slices, cook until golden on each side. Transfer plantains to a paper towel lined plate to soak excess oil. Do this until slices are all cooked.

Combine shredded cheeses together.

To assemble lasagna: Grease bottom and sides of baking pan with butter. Arrange a layer of plantains in baking pan. Top with half of the meat mixture. Top with half of the cheese. Continue layering, starting with plantains and ending with cheese. Pour beaten eggs evenly over top.

Bake uncovered about 30 minutes or until cheese is bubbly. Cool for 10 minutes before cutting and serving.

PATTEN AVENUE CRAB SAUCE WITH ANGEL HAIR PASTA

Serves 4

8 fresh crabs or 2 cups crab meat
2 garlic cloves, chopped finely
¼ cup olive oil
1 tsp. crab seasoning
4 ripe plum tomatoes, diced fine

1 tsp. salt
½ tsp. black pepper
½ pound angel hair pasta
4 chopped parsley sprigs

Rinse crabs with cold water. Put 1 inch water in a large stock pot. When comes to a boil, add the crabs, quickly place the lid on pot and be careful not to get pinched! Steam crabs for 10 minutes, drain water and let cool. When crabs are cool, remove the meat and discard the shells. Put aside.

Heat olive oil in a large sauté pan over medium high flame. When oil is hot add the garlic, sauté for 2 minutes, then add the tomatoes. Cook for 10 minutes, stirring a few times, then add the crab meat, crab seasoning, salt and pepper. Sauté for 2 minutes more, careful not to break up the crab meat. Put to the side until pasta is cooked.

In a large saucepan, bring salted water to a boil. Add the angel hair pasta and cook for 3-5 minutes, until pasta is done. Drain the pasta and reserve a cup of the pasta water.

Plate each pasta dish with the pasta. With a spoon, top the pasta with couple of spoonful's of the crabmeat mixture. Sprinkle parsley over top. Serve with grated cheese.

*Add a little olive oil and some pasta water to keep pasta from sticking.

SHELLS WITH RICOTTA
(Sicilian Style)
Nonno Nino favorite
Serves 4

1 pound large pasta shells
2 cups ricotta cheese

¼ cup grated pecorino romano
salt and pepper to taste

Cook the shells in a large pot in rapidly boiling salted water until al dente.

Meanwhile, in a bowl, combine the ricotta cheese and pecorino cheese. Set aside.

Drain shells. Return to pot and over medium heat add the ricotta cheese mixture and using a wooden spoon, toss together. Cook for a few minutes until warm.

*Additions:

Add 6 cups of marinara sauce to this recipe to make sauce pink, or 2-3 Tsp of truffle oil to make truffle "mac & cheese", Gina's favorite.

HOMEMADE RICOTTA

1 quart heavy cream

½ gallon whole milk

8 x-large or jumbo egg whites, slightly beaten

8 tsp. white wine vinegar

2 tbsp. salt

Place the heavy cream, milk, the lightly beaten eggs, the vinegar and the salt in a deep saucepan. Turn heat to medium/high, then stirring slowly and continuously bring to a slow boil. Lower the flame a bit and continue to stir slowly for approximately 10 or so minutes, until you feel and see the cream thickening and the ricotta rising to the top. Stir slowly, careful not to break up the chunks of ricotta.

Remove from heat, wait 20 minutes, then with a slotted spoon or spatula, scoop the ricotta and put in a colander to drain. Place dish underneath to catch any liquid. Refrigerate to thicken.

RISOTTO PORCINI

Serves 4

1 cup aborio rice	½ cup parmigiano cheese
2 cups chicken stock	¼ onion, finely chopped
2 tbsp. butter	½ cup dried porcini mushrooms
4 tbsp. olive oil	salt and pepper

Soak the mushrooms in 1 cup warm water for 20 minutes.

Squeeze out the liquid, reserving the mushroom water, and chop the mushrooms into small pieces and set aside.

In a large saucepan, over medium heat, melt the butter with the oil. Add the onions and mushrooms and sauté for 5 minutes. Stir in the rice and toss to coat with the butter mixture. Add the reserved mushroom water and stir for 5 minutes. Begin to add chicken stock, half cup at a time, stirring continuously. As the rice absorbs the liquid, add the next ½ cup broth. Continue to stir and adding stock until the rice will no longer absorb the liquid and the rice is cooked. Cook for a total of about 20 minutes. Rice should be a little al dente to the bite.

Serve with parmigiano cheese and a little bit of truffle oil drizzled on top.

Baked Cod with Tomato Coulis
Bouillabaisse
Clams in Green Sauce
Clams Oreganata
Corn Crab Cakes
Fish Tacos
Flounder or Shrimp Francese
Lobster Roll
Lobster Bake
Lobster Mac and Cheese
Paella Alla Maria
Panko-crusted Fish Sticks
Salmon with Red Curry Sauce
Seared Scallops over Lentils
Shrimp Parmigiano
Shrimp Scampi
Swordfish Skewers with Salsa Verde
Zuppa Di Clams

Seafood

BAKED COD WITH TOMATO COULIS

Serves 4

4 fresh cod fillets

4 plum tomatoes, diced small

1 tsp. finely chopped garlic

2 tbsp. of finely chopped onion

4 sprigs parsley, finely chopped

1 tbsp. capers

2 tbsp. chopped green olives

4 tbsp. extra virgin olive

1 tsp. salt

½ tsp. black pepper

¼ cup of seasoned breadcrumbs

To Make the Coulis:

In a bowl, combine the tomatoes, garlic, onion, parsley, capers, green olives, salt, pepper and olive oil. Stir well and let stand at room temperature until ready to use.

Preheat oven to 375 degrees.

To Make the Fish:

Place the Cod fillets on baking pan. Season with a little salt, then spoon the coulis over the top of each fillet. Sprinkle with breadcrumbs and bake for 20-25 minutes until golden on top and fish is cooked.

BOUILLABAISSE – pronounced Boo'-ya-bae
(French Fish Stew from Marseille)

Serves 8

2 lbs. hardy fish fillets*	4 sprigs thyme
3 tbsp. olive oil	2 bay leaves
1 tsp. finely chopped garlic	1 cup dry white wine
1 cup finely chopped onions	1 ¼ tsp. anise seed
2 leeks, ¼ inch cubes	3 ½ cup fish broth (recipe below)
½ cup chopped celery	32 mussels, cleaned and scrubbed
1 tsp. turmeric	8 croutons (see recipe below)
½ tsp. red hot pepper flakes	1 bunch cleaned, chopped parsley
1 cup crushed tomatoes	

* Boneless, skinless hardy fillets like monk fish, tile fish or blackfish. They should be cut in 1 inch cubes.

Heat the oil in a large saucepan and add the garlic and onion. Cook, stirring until wilted then add leek, celery, turmeric, pepper flakes, salt and pepper. Cook over medium heat for about 2 minutes. Add tomatoes, thyme, bay leaf, white wine, Anise seed and fish broth. Bring to a boil and simmer for 15 minutes. Add the fish and mussels and bring back to a boil, then lower flame and simmer for 5 more minutes or until the mussels have opened. Serve in a bowl, each one topped with a crouton and sprinkle with parsley.

Fish Broth: Boil fish bones/fish head, no gills, in 4 cups of water and 1 tbsp. salt and boil for 15 minutes. Strain, discard bones. Can substitute fish stock with shrimp or chicken stock.

Croutons: Use a loaf of French or Italian bread, rub the outside of bread with 1 garlic clove, cut diagonally into 8 slices, about ½ inch thick. Arrange on a cookie tray and brush one side with olive oil, broil until golden, then turn over, brush the other side. Be careful not to burn bread.

CLAMS IN GREEN SAUCE
Serves 4

2 dozen clams
1/3 cup of extra virgin olive oil
½ cup white wine
5 garlic cloves
3 tbsp. green bell pepper

10 parsley sprigs, finely chopped
1 cup water
pinch of red pepper flakes
1 tsp. salt

Place the clams in a large bowl/basin and fill with cold salty water to cover clams. Let soak for about an hour, to expel their sand. Drain the water and rinse them well in running cold tap water.

Finely dice the garlic and green pepper.

In a large, deep sauté pan (large enough to hold all the clams) heat the oil and add the garlic and sauté for about 3 minutes. Then add the green pepper and continue to cook for 5 minutes.

Add the drained clams, wine, water and salt. Stir and cover with a lid, and cook for approximately 10 minutes. You may need to stir a couple times to move them around a bit so they have room to open. When they have all opened, remove from heat and sprinkle with the chopped parsley and red pepper flakes. Discard any that do not open.

Serve with bread to soak up all the delicious broth.

CLAMS OREGANATA

Serves 6

36 fresh littleneck clams

2 cups seasoned breadcrumbs

1 tbsp. minced flat leaf parsley

½ tsp. minced garlic

1 tsp. dried oregano

salt and pepper to taste

½ cup olive oil

¾ cup chicken broth

6 lemon wedges

*If you (or your significant other) don't know how to open clams yourself, ask the fishmonger to open them for you, leaving them on the half shell. Refrigerate until ready to use. You can also steam the clams in ½ inch of water until they open a bit and then remove the one side of the clam shell, keeping the clam on the other side.

Place broiler tray on the lowest rack and preheat broiler.

In a bowl, combine breadcrumbs, parsley, garlic, oregano, salt and pepper. Add the olive oil and toss mixture until crumbs are evenly coated. Add the broth and continue to mix until mixture is very well blended and looks a little wet.

Put approximately 1 heaping tbsp. of breadcrumb mixture on each clam. Smooth over the top, making sure that the edges are sealed.

Place the clams in a large cookie sheet with sides, and pour in 1/8 inch of water (this will keep clams moist while broiling) and broil for about 5-7 minutes or until topping is golden in color. Serve with lemon wedges.

CORN CRAB CAKES
Serves 4

1 lb. lump crabmeat
½ cup canned corn
½ cup diced onion
½ cup diced green pepper
½ cup diced celery
½ cup mayonnaise
½ tsp. dry mustard

1 tsp. old bay seasoning
¼ tsp. cayenne pepper
1 egg (beaten)
1 ½ cups crushed saltine crackers
¼ cup olive oil
3 tbsp. butter

Combine crab, corn, onion, pepper and celery. Toss gently without destroying the lumps of crabmeat.

Combine ½ cup mayonnaise, mustard and cayenne. Gently add to crab mixture with salt and pepper to taste. Fold in egg and ¼ cup cracker crumbs (try not to disturb the crabmeat). Add a bit more mayo if it appears too dry or firm.

Form into 8 patties. Coat with the remaining crumbs and chill 30 minutes.

Heat oil and butter in frying pan and cook cakes on medium heat on both sides until golden brown.

FISH TACOS
Serves 4

1 pound firm white fish*
2 medium limes, halved
1 garlic clove, finely chopped
¼ tsp. chili powder
¼ tsp. cumin
½ small head of red cabbage

½ red onion
¼ cup fresh cilantro, chopped
6-8 soft corn tortillas
olive oil
salt

* Good choices are Mahi Mahi or Grouper.

Prepare the Fish: Cut fish into 3" thick strips, then place on a baking pan and squeeze the juice from ½ a lime on top. Add the garlic, chili powder, cumin and 2 tbsp. of the olive oil, add salt and pepper. Turn the pieces in the marinade until they are evenly coated, cover and refrigerate for at least 20 minutes.

Make the Slaw: Thinly sliced the cabbage and onion. Combine the cabbage, onion and cilantro in a large bowl, and squeeze the other half lime over the mix. Drizzle with 2 tbsp. of olive oil, season with salt and pepper. Toss well and put aside. Taste prior to serving and adjust the salt/lime. Heat the tortillas in a pan, keep warm while making the fish.

Cook the Fish: Use a grill pan or outdoor grill, brush the grates with oil first, then turn on heat and when grill is very hot, place the fish pieces on hot grill. Cook for 3-5 minutes on each side, turning only once. Transfer the fish to a plate.

For Garnishes:
sliced avocado/guacamole
sour cream

salsa
salsa picante

To assemble the tacos, place some fish in a warm tortilla, and top with slaw and any other garnishes.

FLOUNDER or SHRIMP FRANCESE
Serves 6

2 lbs. flounder or

2 lbs. shrimp, butterflied

1 ½ cups all-purpose flour

4 large eggs (beaten)

½ cup vegetable oil

1 cup chicken stock

juice of 2 lemons

salt and pepper to taste

garlic powder

6 tbsp. of butter

3 tbsp. chopped parsley

Heat oil in a large sauté pan on medium heat. Season the flour with salt, pepper and garlic powder and spread on wax paper. Dredge the fish in the seasoned flour and then dip into egg mixture. When oil is hot, carefully place fish in the pan and brown each side, turning only once, until golden. Do not overcrowd the pieces and cook in batches if you have to. If oil is hot enough, it should take only a minute on each side. Place fish pieces on a warm plate while you prepare the sauce.

Drain off all excess oil and return pan to medium high and add the chicken stock, lemon juice, salt and pepper. Bring to a boil and whisk in the butter until sauce becomes thick. Place fish back into pan, and cook on a low flame for 5 more minutes. Sprinkle with parsley and serve.

HAMPTONS LOBSTER ROLL
Serves 6

3 - 1¼ lb. lobsters

¼ cup finely chopped celery

¼ cup mayonnaise

1 tsp. old bay seasoning

½ tsp. salt

½ tsp. black pepper

6 hot dog buns

Steam the lobsters and remove claws and tails from the shell. Chop the meat into small pieces. The seafood dept. in most grocery stores will steam the lobsters for you at no cost.

In a large bowl, put lobster meat, celery, mayonnaise, Old Bay Seasoning, salt and pepper to taste. Let stand in refrigerator for 15 minutes.

Serve piled into hot dog buns.

Maria Francisco

LOBSTER BAKE
Serves 4

4 lobsters

4 ears of corn

1 package of kielbasa sausage

1 pound jumbo shrimp shell on

8 baby red potatoes

2 tbsp. old bay seasoning

Cook the corn and potatoes in advance. Break corn in half. Cut kielbasa into 3 inch pieces.

In a lobster pot (large enough to hold everything), bring 4 inches of water to a boil. Add the lobsters first, sprinkle the old bay, then layer with shrimp, corn, the potatoes and top with the kielbasa. Place lid and let steam for about 20 minutes or until the lobsters have turned pink and cooked.

LOBSTER MAC AND CHEESE
Serves 6

1 pound elbow macaroni

1 quart milk

8 tbsp. butter

½ cup all-purpose flour

4 cups gruyere cheese, grated

3 cups sharp cheddar, grated

½ tsp. black pepper

½ tsp. nutmeg

1 ½ lb. cooked lobster meat, cut up (about 2 lobsters)

½ cup unseasoned breadcrumbs

Preheat oven to 375 degrees.

Cook pasta by bringing a pot full of water with 1 tbsp. salt to a boil. Add the pasta, stir and continue to cook until al dente, about 6 minutes, then drain pasta well and put aside.

Meanwhile, heat the milk in a small saucepan, but don't boil it, set aside. In a large pot, melt 6 tbsp. butter and add flour. Stir well and cook over low heat for 2 minutes while stirring with a whisk. While whisking, add the hot milk and cook for a minute or two until thickened and smooth. Remove from heat then add the cheeses, 1 tbsp. salt, pepper and nutmeg. Add the cooked macaroni and lobster meat, and stir well. Place the mixture in a deep baking pan.

Melt the remaining 2 tbsp. butter, combine with the breadcrumbs, and sprinkle on top of macaroni.

Bake for 30 minutes or until the pasta is golden brown on the top.

PAELLA ALLA MARIA
Serves 4

4 skin-on chicken thighs, halved

4 garlic cloves, finely chopped

1 large onion, chopped

2 chorizo sausages, chopped

large pinch of saffron

1 small jar of red pimentos

1/2 cup olive oil

1 small jar of olives with pimento

1 cup frozen peas

8 cups of chicken stock

4 cups of long grain rice

4 bay leaves

18 small littleneck clams, steamed

1 pound large shrimp

1 pound calamari ringlets

1 pound bay scallops

2 lobsters, steamed

12 mussels steamed

In a very large pot (big enough to hold all ingredients) on medium flame, sauté chicken with oil, garlic, onion and chorizo. When chicken is browned on both sides, add peas and rice. Coat the rice then add the stock, bay leaf, and saffron. Bring to a boil then lower the flame, stir well and place lid. Let cook unstirred for 20 minutes.

Remove lid, add olives, pimentos, shrimp, scallops, calamari, and clams. Mix in everything and cook for 10 minutes more with the lid on. Add lobsters cut in half still in their shells and serve.

PANKO-CRUSTED FISH STICKS
Serves 4

1 tbsp. milk

2 large eggs, beaten

1 pound halibut fillets

1 cup panko

1 tsp. salt

1 tsp. black pepper

¼ cup vegetable oil

¼ cup sour cream

3 tbsp. mayonnaise

2 tbsp. finely chopped bread-and-butter pickles or relish

2 tsp. minced capers

Combine milk and eggs in a large bowl, stir with a whisk. Cut fish into 20 1 inch strips. Add fish to milk mixture and toss gently to coat. Place panko, salt and pepper in a large zip-top bag. Add fish to panko mixture, seal bag and shake bag gently to coat fish.

In a large non-stick skillet, heat half of the oil in pan over medium high heat. When oil is hot, add half the fish, cook 4 minutes or until golden, turning occasionally to brown all sides. Repeat procedure with the other half of the fish.

Dipping Sauce:

In a small bowl, combine sour cream, mayonnaise, pickles, capers, salt and pepper. Serve sauce with fish.

Maria Francisco

SALMON WITH RED CURRY SAUCE
Serves 6

6 salmon pieces
6 tbsp. olive oil

garlic powder
salt and pepper to taste

Preheat oven to 400 degrees. Prepare salmon pieces on a large baking sheet and sprinkle each with garlic powder, salt and pepper. Drizzle each piece with 1 tbsp. olive oil and bake for 20 minutes, then broil for 5 minutes until top is crispy, careful not to burn.

Red Curry Sauce:

1 can (15 oz.) coconut milk
2 tbsp. Red Curry Paste

1 tbsp. brown sugar
1 tsp. fish sauce *optional

In a saucepan, bring the coconut milk to a simmer and add the red curry paste and the brown sugar (and the fish sauce if using it). Bring to a boil and simmer for 5 minutes. Put aside.

Place cooked salmon pieces on serving platter and pour the red curry sauce over each piece. Serve with Jasmine Rice.

SEARED SCALLOPS OVER LENTILS
Serves 4

20 fresh sea scallops
1 ½ cups green lentils
3 cups chicken stock
1 small tomato, diced fine
3 tbsp. olive oil

3 tbsp. olive oil (for pan searing)
4 ginger slices
1- 2" lemon peel strip
salt and garlic powder, to taste

Rinse lentils and place in pot, add the olive oil and stock and cook for 10 minutes. Add the diced tomato, ginger slices and lemon strip. Continue cooking for 15 minutes more, until lentils are soft and tender. Let cool for a few minutes, then pour half the lentils into a blender and puree. Add back to the pot and mix well into the other whole lentil mixture. Keep warm until ready to serve.

Meanwhile, dry each scallop with a paper towel. Season them with a little salt and garlic powder. Then using a large sauté pan, add olive oil to the bottom and heat over medium flame and when oil is hot, sear scallops 3-4 minutes on each side.

*Be careful not to overcrowd the scallops in the pan or they won't sear correctly. Work in batches if you have to.

Prepare the dish by putting the lentils on the bottom of the plate and place the seared scallops on top. Serve hot.

Maria Francisco

SHRIMP PARMIGIANO
Serves 6

24 jumbo shrimp
1- ½ cup seasoned breadcrumbs
½ cup grated parmigiano cheese
3 eggs (beaten)
1 bag of shredded mozzarella

2 cups tomato sauce pg. 63
¼ cup olive oil
¼ vegetable oil
1 tsp. salt
1 tsp. black pepper

Preheat oven to 400 degrees.

Peel and devein shrimp, leaving tails on, and butterfly.

In a large flat plate, mix the breadcrumbs, grated cheese, salt and pepper. In a large bowl, beat the eggs. Then take a shrimp, spread open, dip in the egg mixture and then dip in the breadcrumbs.

In a large frying pan, heat the olive oil and the vegetable oil until hot. Add the shrimp, be sure to fan out the shrimp so that they are flat and open like a fan, (be careful not to overcrowd) and cook a couple minutes on each side until golden color. Place cooked shrimp on a baking tray. Top with 2 tbsp. of tomato sauce and 1 tbsp. of shredded mozzarella cheese.

Bake in oven for 5-10 minutes until mozzarella has melted. *Or put under the broiler for few minutes, but be careful not to burn.

Serve with linguini pasta.

SHRIMP SCAMPI

Serves 4

1 pound extra-large shrimp

3 tbsp. italian dry rub, pg. 144

½ tsp. salt

½ tsp. black pepper

2 tbsp. olive oil

4 tbsp. butter, cubed

2 garlic cloves, minced

½ cup white wine

¼ cup fresh lemon juice

1 tbsp. chopped fresh parsley

Peel and devein shrimp. Place the shrimp in a medium bowl and toss with 3 tbsps. Italian dry rub, salt and pepper. Make sure to coat the shrimp well.

Place the olive oil and 1 tbsp. of the butter in a large sauté pan over medium high heat. Add the shrimp and spread them out evenly in the skillet. Cook for 2 minutes then quickly turn to cook other side. Add the garlic and cook for 30 seconds. Add the white wine and lemon juice and cook for 3 minutes, stirring often. Add the remaining 3 tbsp. of butter and season with salt and pepper to taste. Add the parsley and stir to combine.

Serve immediately with plain or jasmine rice.

SWORDFISH SKEWERS WITH SALSA VERDE
Serves 4

1 cup flat leaf parsley leaves

4 garlic cloves, crushed

1 tsp. crushed red pepper

½ cup extra virgin olive oil

1 tsp. salt

½ tsp. black pepper

28 fresh bay leaves

1 ½ pounds of swordfish, cut into 1 ½ " pieces

2 medium zucchini

2 lemons, halved crosswise

In a blender, pulse the parsley, garlic, crushed red pepper, salt, pepper and olive oil to a thick puree. Transfer the sauce to a bowl.

Onto each of 4 long skewers, alternately thread a bay leaf, a piece of fish, another bay leaf and a slice of zucchini folded in two. Repeating until each skewer has 3 pieces of fish, 3 slices of zucchini and 7 bay leaves. Season each piece with salt and pepper and brush all over with the parsley sauce. Cover and refrigerate for 1 hour.

Light a grill or heat a grill pan. Grill skewers over moderate heat, turning until the fish is lightly browned and cooked through, about 6 minutes. Transfer to a platter. Meanwhile, grill the lemon halves cut side down until charred, about 2 minutes. Serve the skewers with the grilled lemons. Discard the bay leaves

ZUPPA DI CLAMS
(Vongole)
Serves 8

36 fresh littleneck clams

¼ cup extra virgin olive oil

4 garlic cloves, peeled & crushed

1 28 oz. can peeled plum tomatoes

4 cups bottled clam juice

½ cup white wine

½ tsp. dried oregano

crushed red pepper, to taste

1 chicken bouillon cube

fresh parsley

In a large bowl filled with cold water, soak the clams for few minutes to release any sand. Then under cold running water, scrub each one with a scrub brush or sponge. Rinse in a colander and drain any excess water.

Drain the tomatoes well and crush them. Heat the oil in a large heavy saucepan over medium heat. Add the garlic, sauté for a minute until golden, add clams. Add tomatoes, wine, clam juice, red pepper flakes and the oregano. Raise the flame and bring to a boil, then lower to a simmer and cook for about 8 minutes until liquid begins to reduce.

Cover with a lid and simmer for a few more minutes until all the clams are open. (Discard any unopened clams)

Sprinkle with parsley and serve with crusty bread.

Beef Stew
Beef Wellington
Berkshire Pork Chops Murphy
Best Meatballs Ever
Braciola
Chicken Cacciatore
Chicken Lascia Me Stare
Chicken Parmigiana
Chicken Savoy
Chicken Scarpiello
Crown Roast or Rack of Lamb with Couscous
Florentine Steak
Holiday Baked Ham
Kielbasa, Pork Chops, Sauerkraut and Onions
Lemon Chicken
Meatloaf, Sicilian Style
Osso Buco
Pernil
Picadillo
Pork Chops with Hot and Sweet Peppers
Roast Chicken
Ropa Vieja
Stuffed Chicken Breast
Thanksgiving Turkey
Veal Cutlets
Veal Milanese
Veal or Chicken Marsala

Meat

BEEF STEW
Serves 6

2 pounds chuck or sirloin steak
½ cup flour
1 cup red wine
1 cup beef stock
2 tbsp. tomato paste

¼ cup olive oil
1 cup chopped onion
4 carrots (cut into 2" pieces)
4 potatoes, quartered

Cut meat into 2 inch pieces. Season flour with salt, pepper and garlic powder. In a bowl, place the meat pieces and sprinkle with the flour mixture. Rub flour onto each individual piece until flour is absorbed into the beef.

In a large pot, heat oil over medium heat and when it's hot, add the meat pieces. Sear the beef on both sides and then add the onion, carrots and tomato paste. Mix well and add the wine, stirring to make sure that the bottom doesn't stick. After few minutes, add the stock, salt and pepper to taste. Bring to a boil, lower flame and simmer for 1 hour, stirring occasionally so meat doesn't stick to bottom of pot. Add the potatoes and let simmer for another half hour or until potatoes are cooked. Serve with white rice or noodles.

BEEF WELLINGTON
(Filet Mignon cooked in Pastry Shell)
Serves 4

4 – 6oz. filet mignon pieces

4 puff pastry sheets

1 cup of sliced mushrooms

3 spanish onions, thinly sliced

½ cup crumbled gorgonzola

½ cup red wine

¼ cup sherry

1 cup steamed spinach

¼ cup oil

¼ stick butter

1 tsp. thyme

salt and pepper to taste

Preheat oven to 400 degrees.

In large pan melt the butter and the oil and sauté the onions on medium flame. When the onions are starting to get a golden color, add the sherry and continue cooking until onions are caramelized and most of the liquid is gone. Let cool and refrigerate for at least an hour.

In the same pan, add a little bit of oil and sear the mushrooms. Season with salt and pepper, let cool then place in refrigerator.

Season the filet mignon pieces with salt and pepper and in a hot pan coated with olive oil, sear the filet pieces on high flame for about 3 minutes on each side and edges. Let cool and refrigerate 3 hours.

Take a pastry sheet, and 2/3 of the way down, place the filet mignon. Top each with a spoonful of the onions, mushrooms and the spinach. Season with salt and pepper and fold the pastry sheet over and secure all around by pressing pastry together. Brush the tops with egg and water wash*. Bake for 30 minutes (for rare/medium rare meat).

* Egg and water wash is 1 egg beaten with 2 tbsp. water.

BERKSHIRE PORK CHOPS MURPHY

Paul's Recipe

Serves 2

2 bone-in berkshire pork chops

8 baby red potatoes

3 sprigs fresh rosemary

½ red onion, thin sliced

1 garlic clove, chopped fine

½ red bell pepper, sliced thin

6 oz. sliced banana peppers

3 oz. olive oil

4 pats of butter

¼ tsp. salt and pepper to taste

Cut potatoes in half and par boil.

Preheat oven to 400 degrees.

Fill a pot with water and 1 tsp. salt and cook potatoes until tender, approximately 8-10 minutes. Drain, cool then cut potatoes in half and set aside.

In a large cast iron frying pan, or pan that can be put into oven, heat olive oil. Add rosemary sprigs and sauté for 2 minutes to release essence, then remove sprigs and add red pepper, onions, and garlic. Sauté for 3-5 minutes until the vegetables are soft. Add the banana peppers with their juice, add potatoes and sauté for 2 minutes. Remove the mixture from pan and put aside.

Add 2 tbsp. of olive oil to the pan and sear the pork chops on high, 2 minutes on each side. Remove from pan, lower the flame, and place half of the vegetable mixture on the bottom of pan. Place the pork chops on top. Top the chops with pats of butter, then place the remaining vegetable mixture on top. Roast in the oven for 10 minutes.

Let sit for a few minutes before serving.

BEST MEATBALLS EVER

Yields Approximately 30 Meatballs

1 pound ground beef

½ pound ground veal

½ pound ground pork

2 large eggs

1 cup grated pecorino romano

2 cups seasoned breadcrumbs

½ cup lukewarm water

2 garlic cloves, chopped fine

4 tbsp. chopped parsley

½ cup fine olive oil

1 tsp. salt ½ tsp. pepper

*Can use 2lb. ground beef instead of pork and veal.

In a large bowl, combine the ground beef, veal and pork. Add the eggs, cheese, parsley, garlic, salt and pepper, and with your hands, mix it all together. Add the breadcrumbs into the mixture slowly and add some of the water a little at a time. This will allow the breadcrumbs to soak it up, making the mixture moist.

Shape meatballs into balls, my family likes them on the smaller side, about 2 ½ inches in diameter.

In a large frying pan, heat the oil. When the oil is hot, add the meatballs and brown them until they are brown and crispy on the one side, then flip over to brown and crisp on the other side. Remove from heat until you are ready to put them into your sauce.

*I usually prepare my sauce alongside, so I can take the meatballs right from the frying pan and put them in the sauce. Allow them to cook and simmer in the tomato sauce for 30 minutes or longer if you have other meat in the sauce.

Maria Francisco

BRACIOLA pronounced BRA-SHOLE
(Sicilian Style)
Nonna Sara's Recipe
Yields 8 Pieces

8 large slices of bottom round beef, cut into
  ¼" thick slices or 8 large slices of pork
8 hardboiled eggs, de-shelled
4 italian sausages, meat out of casing
2 large onions, thinly sliced

½ cup pecorino romano cheese
½ cup flat leaf parsley, chopped
salt and pepper
toothpicks or cooking twine
olive oil

*Can use either beef or pork.

Lay beef slices flat and generously sprinkle each with cheese and parsley. Then 2/3 way down, place a few slices of onion, cooked egg, and sausage meat. Fold sides in then roll up meat like a cigar, keeping it firmly closed using toothpicks or cooking twine.

Heat olive oil in sauté pan over medium heat and when oil is hot, add the meat rolls and brown on all sides.

At this point you can add the Braciola to your Sunday meat sauce with meatballs and sausage or to marinara sauce.

CHICKEN CACCIATORE
(Sweet and Sour Chicken, Sicilian Style)
Grandma Josie's Recipe
Serves 8

2 ½ lbs. chicken pieces

1 cup onion, chopped

1 cup celery, chopped

¼ cup capers

1 cup pitted green pimento olives

1 cup canned sliced mushrooms

¼ cup olive oil

1 cup red wine vinegar

28 oz. tomato sauce

¾ cup sugar

1 tbsp. salt

1 tsp. black pepper

Remove skin from the chicken and boil the chicken pieces in water with 2 tbsp. salt, until chicken is cooked, about 30 minutes. Drain and let cool. Once cool, remove bones and set aside.

Use a large sauté pot (that can hold all of the chicken pieces), pour some olive oil and sauté celery until translucent, remove vegetables to a bowl. Add more oil and sauté the onion for few minutes. Then add back the celery, and add the olives (cut in half), capers and mushrooms (optional). Mix well and cook for few minutes, stirring occasionally so nothing sticks to bottom of pan. Add the tomato sauce to the pot, stir well. Mix the sugar and vinegar in a cup until sugar dissolved and add to the pot. Cook for 5 minutes. Add the chicken pieces to the pot, and simmer for 10-15, stir occasionally, making sure nothing sticks to the bottom of the pot.

Let sit for an hour before serving.

CHICKEN " LASCIA ME STARE "
(Chicken "Leave Me Alone")
Because all you have to do is bake it, no fuss
Nonna Sara's Recipe
Serves 6

1 whole chicken, cut into 8 pieces

1 green bell pepper , sliced ¼ inch

1 red bell pepper , sliced ¼ inch

1 medium/large onion sliced

3 whole garlic cloves

4 rosemary sprigs

¼ cup olive oil

2 tbsp. salt

1 tsp. black pepper

Preheat oven to 375 degrees.

In a deep baking pan, place chicken pieces, sprinkle with a little salt, then top with the peppers, onion, garlic cloves, rosemary, and pepper. Pour the olive oil over everything and toss so all gets coated and well mixed.

Spread everything out evenly in pan, cover with tin foil and bake in oven for 30 minutes. Remove the foil, stir the chicken pieces and continue to cook for another 30 minutes.

CHICKEN PARMIGIANA

Serves 6

2 pounds chicken cutlets

3 large eggs, beaten

3 cups seasoned breadcrumbs

1 tsp. salt

½ tsp. black pepper

½ cup olive oil

½ vegetable oil

1 cup grated parmigiano cheese

½ lb. fresh mozzarella, sliced thin

1 qt. tomato sauce, pg. 59

Preheat oven 450 degrees.

Beat the eggs in a wide shallow bowl, and in another wide shallow bowl, mix the breadcrumbs with a ½ cup of grated Parmigiano cheese, salt and pepper, mix, then place bowls next to each other.

Take a chicken cutlet and dip in the egg, then coat with the breadcrumbs on both sides. Shake off any excess breadcrumbs. Repeat until all the pieces of chicken are coated.

Combine ½ cup olive oil with the ½ cup vegetable oil.

Pour half the oil in a sauté pan, and when oil is very hot, cook chicken cutlets until golden, about 2 minutes on each side, cooking in batches and adding oil as needed, until all the chicken cutlets are cooked.

Place the chicken pieces side by side in a large baking pan and top each piece with a couple heaping tbsp. of sauce. Spread the sauce a bit, then top each piece of chicken with a mozzarella slice, sprinkle a layer of the parmigiano cheese on top and drizzle with little olive oil.

Bake in heated oven until cheese is browned and bubbly, approximately 15 minutes. Let sit for few minutes before serving.

CHICKEN SAVOY

Serves 6

1 whole chicken cut into pieces	3 large garlic cloves, crushed
½ cup of olive oil	¼ cup grated pecorino romano
1 cup chicken stock	¼ cup balsamic vinegar
¼ cup of dried oregano	salt and pepper

Preheat oven to 450 degrees.

Place chicken pieces in pan, sprinkle each piece with salt and pepper on both sides. Pour olive oil over pieces, add chicken stock, garlic and the oregano. Toss lightly to coat each chicken piece. Top chicken pieces with the cheese and cook for 60 minutes or until chicken is nice and roasted.

Remove from oven, pour the balsamic vinegar over chicken and serve.

CHICKEN SCARPIELLO
(Means Shoemaker Style)
Serves 4

16 oz. italian sausage links

6 chicken thighs, skinless

1 cup balsamic vinegar

½ stick of butter

1 cup of chicken stock

¼ cup of vegetable oil

15 oz. can sliced mushrooms

3 crushed garlic cloves

2 tbsp. dried oregano

½ cup of all-purpose flour

Preheat oven to 375 degrees.

Cut the chicken and sausages pieces in half. Season flour with salt, pepper and garlic powder and put in a bowl.

In a large sauté pan, heat the oil until hot. Dredge chicken pieces in the seasoned flour, shake off excess flour, then place into the frying pan. Add the sausage to the pan side-by-side with the chicken pieces. Brown the chicken and the sausage on both sides. When browned, remove them and place in a large baking pan, big enough to hold all the pieces. Continue until all the pieces have been browned.

Discard the oil from the frying pan and return it to medium heat. Add the chicken stock, scraping the bottom and sides, bring to a boil, then pour over chicken/sausage pieces. Add the butter to the same pan. Once the butter has melted, add the balsamic vinegar and cook on medium heat, stirring until sauce reduces and gets thick; about 5 minutes. Then pour over the chicken/sausage pieces. Add the mushrooms, garlic and the oregano to the baking pan. The liquid should come up half way, if not, add a little more chicken stock. Give it a good stir and bake in oven uncovered for approximately 45 minutes or until chicken pieces are done. Let stand for a few minutes before serving. Serve with bread for dunking!

*Can be made the day before.

CROWN ROAST OR RACK OF LAMB WITH COUSCOUS

Serves 4

1 3 lb crown roast of lamb, prepared by a
  butcher or 2 racks of lamb, frenched
1 cup seasoned breadcrumbs
3 tbsp. minced garlic
3 tbsp. chopped fresh rosemary

¼ cup olive oil
2 tsp. salt
½ tsp. black pepper
2 cups prepared couscous

Preheat oven to 450 degrees.

If making the crown roast, position baking rack at lower level in the oven so the crown will have room on the top, otherwise if making the racks of lamb, place rack in center of oven.

In a large bowl, combine the breadcrumbs, garlic, rosemary, salt and pepper. Toss in the olive oil to moisten the mixture and set aside.

Season the crown roast or lamb racks with a little salt and pepper then roll in the breadcrumb mixture until evenly coated. Cover the ends of the bones with foil to prevent charring.

In a large heavy oven proof skillet or baking pan, place the crown upright in the center of the pan. If making the racks, place them upright, leaning on each other, with bones intertwined so they are standing up.

Roast the lamb in preheated oven for about 15-20 minutes, depending on the degree of doneness you want. Use a meat thermometer to determine if it's cooked to the right temperature. When cooked, remove from oven and let rest for 5-10 minutes, loosely covered with tin foil, before carving between the ribs. (It will continue to cook for a few minutes more while it's resting)

Place the Crown Roast on a serving platter and fill the center of the crown with the couscous prepared as per instructions on the box. If making the lamb racks, carve the racks by slicing between each rib bone and make chops. Place chops over couscous and serve.

FLORENTINE STEAK

Serves 6

6 16-oz. porterhouse steaks*
salt and pepper to taste
florentine rub: pg.139

For the Salad:
bunch of arugula
1 tomato cut into small pieces

2 tbsp. chopped onion
½ tsp. salt
¼ tsp. black pepper
1 tsp. dried oregano
¼ cup extra virgin olive oil
1/8 cup balsamic vinegar

*Can use New York strip steaks instead.

Prepare the steaks by sprinkling with salt and pepper, then rub each side of the steak with 1 heaping tbsp. of the rub. Let sit until ready to grill.

Meanwhile prepare the salad. In a bowl, combine the tomatoes, onion, salt, black pepper, oregano, olive oil and vinegar. Let stand at room temperature until ready to serve. Spread the arugula salad on a serving platter, and put aside.

Heat the grill, when grill is hot, cook the steaks 4 minutes on each side, turning twice, until meat is desired temperature. Remove from heat and let stand for 5 minutes, then slice meat.

Pour the dressing over the arugula, then place sliced steak on top and serve.

HOLIDAY BAKED HAM
Serves 12

1 Spiral-sliced half ham
20 oz. can sliced pineapple

¾ cup packed light brown sugar
2 tbsp. yellow mustard

Preheat oven to 350 degrees

Make the Glaze:

In a small bowl, combine the brown sugar, mustard and a little pineapple juice from the can to make a thick glaze. Put aside.

Place ham in a baking pan and bake in oven for 30 minutes. Remove from oven and spoon the glaze all over the ham. Then arrange pineapple slices all over the ham and secure with toothpicks. Place ham back in the oven and continue cooking, uncovered for another 30 minutes.

Take ham out of the oven and remove the pineapple slices and toothpicks. Transfer to platter or cutting board and carve.

KIELBASA, PORK CHOPS, SAUERKRAUT AND ONIONS
Paul's Polish Family's Recipe
Serves 6

4 pork chops

2 pounds polish kielbasa, cut diagonally
   into 1" slices

2 large onions, sliced thin

4 tbsp. butter

4 tbsp. olive oil

2 pounds sauerkraut, strained

Cut each pork chop into 3 pieces. Slice the kielbasa diagonally into 1 inch slices.

In a large sauté pan, heat the oil and butter on medium flame, add the onion and sauté for approximately 5-10 minutes until onions become translucent and slightly browned. Then add the sauerkraut and sauté for an additional 5 minutes. Remove from pan and put aside. In the same pan, cook the kielbasa for a few minutes until browned and put aside with the onions and sauerkraut. Then add the pork chop pieces and continue to cook for 10 minutes or so, browning them on both sides. Once browned, add back the onions, sauerkraut, and kielbasa and mix well together. Continue cooking for another 10 minutes. Serve with brown mustard and potatoes.

LEMON CHICKEN

Serves 6

1 2 ½ - 3 pound chicken, halved
  or 8 pieces of chicken
1 cup fresh lemon juice
½ cup olive oil

1 tsp. red wine vinegar
1 tsp. minced garlic
1 tsp. oregano
salt and pepper to taste

Wisk together the lemon juice, vinegar, garlic, oregano, salt and pepper. Cover and put to side until ready to use. Wisk vigorously when ready to use.

Preheat broiler for 10 minutes so it's nice and hot. Broil the chicken halves, for about 30 minutes, turning only once after the first 15 min, or until skin is golden brown and chicken is cooked. Be careful not to burn.

Remove the chicken from broiler, leaving the broiler on, and with a sharp knife, cut each half into 4 pieces. Place chicken pieces on a baking pan with sides, so that the juice doesn't run off. Pour lemon sauce over the chicken and toss well to coat. Return to broiler and broil for 3 minutes, then turn the pieces and broil for another 3 minutes.

Remove from broiler and portion each chicken pieces on warm serving plates.

Pour sauce into a saucepan. Stir in parsley and cook on high heat for a minute. Pour over chicken pieces and serve with crusty bread to soak up all the delicious juice.

MEATLOAF
(Sicilian Style)
Nonna Sara's Recipe
Serves 8

2 pounds ground beef	2 hard-boiled eggs
4 italian sausage links	½ cup grated romano cheese
1 small onion, sliced thin	1 tsp. salt
2 eggs	1 tsp. black pepper
1 cup seasoned breadcrumbs	¼ cup warm water

Preheat oven to 350 degrees.

In a large bowl, combine ground beef, 2 eggs, breadcrumbs, grated cheese, salt and pepper, and water. Mix well with your hands.

Take 2/3 of the meat mixture and shape into a log about 4 inches wide and as long as the pan, then place log in baking pan. Make a lengthwise indentation in the center of the log about 2 inches deep, leaving the sides 1 inch wide. Take the sausage meat out of its casing and spread evenly in the indentation. Place a layer of onion on top of the sausage meat. Cut the hardboiled eggs in half, lengthwise and place into the onion and sausage.

Take the remaining meat mixture and flatten it out and shape it so it covers the top of the log. Seal sides of the bottom and top of the ground meat together, so sausage mixture is contained on the inside.

Bake for 45 minutes, uncovered. Let rest a few minutes before slicing.

OSSO BUCO VEAL SHANKS
(Means Bone With a Hole)
Serves 6

1 cup finely chopped onion	8 pieces of veal shanks, 2" thick
2/3 cup finely chopped carrot	¾ cup flour
2/3 cup finely chopped celery	1 cup dry white wine
¼ cup butter	2 cups meat broth
2 tbsp. finely chopped garlic	1 ½ cups chopped tomatoes
2 strips of lemon peel	2 bay leaves
½ cup vegetable oil	Salt and pepper to taste

*Can use beef shanks instead of veal.

Preheat oven to 350 degrees.

Choose a heavy casserole dish, large enough to contain the meat pieces in a single layer. In a pan, melt the butter and sauté the onion, carrots and celery, cook over medium heat for 8-10 minutes, then place in the casserole dish and spread it out to cover the bottom. Add the garlic and the lemon peel.

Heat the oil in a skillet on medium/high heat. Season flour with salt and pepper and put on wax paper. Dredge the meat pieces in the flour, one by one, coating all the sides and shaking off any excess flour. When the oil is hot, brown the meat on all sides. Place the meat pieces side-by-side on top of the vegetables.

Tip the skillet and draw off most of the fat with a spoon. Add the wine and boil for 3 minutes, scraping up and loosening any browning residue stuck to pan. Pour over meat pieces.

In the same skillet, bring the broth to a simmer and pour over into the casserole dish. Add the chopped tomatoes and their juices, bay leaves, salt and pepper. The broth should come to the top of the meat pieces, otherwise add more. Cover tightly with tin foil and cook for 3 hours.

PERNIL
(Puerto Rican Style)
Serves 8-10

1 5-8 lb. whole pork shoulder
5 garlic cloves
1tbsp. garlic powder
1tbsp. onion powder

2 tbsp. brown sugar
1 tsp. salt
1 tsp. black pepper
1 cup prepared l'ansolio pg. 142

Preheat oven to 325 degrees.

Place the meat in a large roasting pan. With a pointy knife, make 5 deep holes (about 1" deep), shove the garlic pieces in the holes.

Prepare dry rub by combining garlic powder, onion powder, brown sugar, salt and pepper. Rub the meat with some olive oil and then sprinkle the dry rub on it, and rub it all over. Pour 1 cup of water or white wine into the bottom of the pan. Cover the meat loosely with foil paper and bake in oven for 5-6 hours, depending on size. Baste occasionally with its own juice and add liquid as needed. The meat is done when it falls apart with a fork.

Meanwhile, prepare the L'ansoglio.

After meat has cooked, let sit for about 10 minutes. While it's still warm, place meat on cutting board and carve into slices or shred it with a fork, then return to the pan and add the L'ansoglio. Toss meat well so that it's evenly coated. Transfer to a large platter that can hold the meat with its juice and serve.

*Make Cuban sandwiches with the leftover meat

PICADILLO
(Cuban Recipe)
Serves 4

1 pound ground beef

1 green pepper, finely chopped

1 medium onion, finely chopped

4 garlic cloves, minced

2 tsp. salt

½ cup pimento stuffed olives

½ cup beef stock or wine

½ tsp. black pepper

1 tsp. salt

1 tsp. cumin

1 tsp. oregano

2 bay leaves

1-8oz. can tomato sauce

½ cup ketchup

2 small potatoes, diced small

4 tbsp. olive oil

In a pot, heat 1 tbsp. of the olive oil and add the beef. Cook for few minutes until the meat is browned. Remove the meat from the pot, drain the fat and place the meat in bowl. Season with the oregano, cumin, salt and pepper.

In the same pot, heat 3 tbsp. of olive oil, add the green pepper, onion and garlic. Sauté 10 minutes then add the meat back, and add the other ingredients. Bring to a boil, reduce heat, cover and simmer for 20 minutes, add potatoes and continue to cook for another 20 minutes. Serve with white rice.

*To make "Picadillo a Caballo" place a fried egg on top of picadillo and rice. Can also be used for meat empanada stuffing.

PORK CHOPS WITH VINEGARED HOT AND SWEET PEPPERS

Serves 4

6- 1" thick pork chops
½ cup olive oil
½ cup white wine
$^1/_3$ cup marinated hot peppers
½ cup marinated sweet peppers

1/3 cup of the vinegar juice from the peppers
6 small baby potatoes
1 small onion, sliced
salt and pepper to taste
1garlic clove, peeled

Boil the baby potatoes in salted water until done. Drain, let cool then cut in half, put aside.

In a large sauté pan, big enough to hold the pork chops, heat the oil. When the oil is hot, put in the garlic then sprinkle the pork chops with salt and black pepper. Place in the pan.

Fry over medium heat for 3-5 minutes on each side, turning once, until they are nicely browned. Remove the garlic. When pork chops are cooked, remove from pan, drain off all excess oil, and transfer them to a plate.

Cut the cherry peppers in half, remove any seeds. Measure out 1/3 cup vinegar juice and put aside.

Return pan to medium heat, add the chops, peppers, onion, wine and vinegar to the pan. Season with a little salt and pepper and cook for about 10 minutes, stirring occasionally so nothing sticks, then add the potatoes, mix and cook for another 5 minutes. Serve.

Maria Francisco

BEST EVER ROASTED CHICKEN

Serves 4

3 ½ pound whole chicken
3 rosemary sprig, chopped fine
6 sprigs of thyme, chopped fine
8 sprigs parsley, chopped fine
4 tbsp. butter, softened

½ tsp. salt
¼ tsp. ground black pepper
1 garlic head, split horizontally
3 tbsp. olive oil

Preheat oven to 450 degrees.

In a small bowl, combine half the rosemary, thyme, parsley, salt and pepper with the softened butter. Use a fork to blend the herbs with the butter.

Going through the neck opening of the chicken, slide your fingers between the skin and the breast, separating the two, then slide the herbed butter under the skin of both breasts, careful not to rip through. Stuff the cavity with the remaining chopped herbs and the garlic. Truss the chicken (tie the legs together) with twine or thread. Season with salt and pepper

Over high flame, heat the olive oil in a heavy ovenproof sauté pan or roasting pan, until it smokes. Place the bird on its side, searing the leg and breast. Leave it untouched in the pan for a least 4 minutes, turning only when the bird is browned. Turn to brown the other breast side, and then top and bottom of the bird so that it is well-browned on all sides.

Place the pan in the oven. Cook for 40-45 minutes, basting occasionally. If the chicken skin begins to burn, cover with an aluminum foil tent for the remainder of the cooking time.

ROPA VIEJA
(Means "Old Clothes" Cuban Recipe)
Serves 6

2 ½ pounds beef flank steak

1 cup beef broth

1- 8 oz. can tomato sauce

1 onion

1 green bell pepper

3 garlic cloves, chopped fine

2 tbsp. tomato paste

3 tbsp. sofrito

1 tsp. cumin

3 tbsp. olive oil

1 bay leaf

1 small jar of pimento strips

1 tbsp. salt

1 tsp. black pepper

In a large pot, filled half way with water, add the salt and the flank steak. Cook on high flame, and when water comes to a boil, lower the flame and place a lid on pot. Simmer for an hour. Remove the meat and discard the water. Let the meat sit for few minutes to cool off. Then using two forks, shred the meat. Set the meat aside.

Finely chop the onion and pepper. In the pot, heat the olive oil, add the onion, garlic, green pepper, and Sofrito. Sauté for few minutes, then stir in the tomato paste, add shredded meat, beef stock, tomato sauce, cumin, and bay leaf. Let simmer for 30 minutes, then add the drained pimentos and let cook for an additional 5 minutes. Serve with white rice and black beans.

STUFFED CHICKEN BREAST
Serves 4

4 boneless chicken breasts
½ lb. sliced ham, sliced thick
½ lb. provolone, sliced thick
16 ounce bag spinach
2 cups seasoned breadcrumbs

1 tsp. salt
½ tsp. black pepper
1 tsp. garlic powder
½ cup butter, melted
3 tbsp. olive oil

Preheat oven to 350 degrees.

Slice each chicken breast across the middle to make 8 pieces. On a cutting board, pound chicken breasts until they are thin and wide.

In a small pan, cook the spinach along with the olive oil, salt and pepper until done.

To assemble the stuffed chicken breast, take a chicken cutlet, then place a slice of ham on top, then a slice of the provolone cheese and a heaping tbsp. of the spinach. Then fold one side over, kind of like a taco, make sure to tuck in any pieces of ham/cheese that might be sticking out, and secure with a toothpick.

Roll each chicken breast in bread crumbs until well coated. Place in a glass baking dish, with seam side down, and pour butter over them. Bake uncovered for 30 minutes.

*Make sure to remove any toothpicks before serving.

TRADITIONAL THANKSGIVING TURKEY WITH STUFFING

Mamie's Recipe

Serves 12

12-15 lb. turkey, fresh preferred
1 stick salted butter, softened
2 tsp. finely chopped rosemary
2 tsp. finely chopped thyme

FOR THE STUFFING:
½ pound ground beef

1 lb. ground italian sausage
1 12 oz. roll pork breakfast sausage, thawed
1celery stalks, chopped
1 large onion, chopped
1 cup finely chopped carrots
12-14 oz. seasoned stuffing cubes
2 cups chicken broth

Preheat Oven to 350 degrees.

Combine butter with rosemary and thyme in a bowl. Using your fingers, beginning at the neck of the turkey, separate the skin from the breast meat. Spread the herbed butter in between the skin and meat and spread all over, careful not to break through skin.

Prepare Stuffing

In a large skillet, brown the sausages and ground beef together over medium heat for about 5 minutes, then add the celery, onions and carrots. Cook and stir for another 10 minutes. Put the meat in a large bowl and add the stuffing cubes, stir in broth and toss well.

Stuff the turkey in the stomach cavity and the neck, (make sure you removed the organs that are typically in the cavity). Place the turkey in a strong, deep roasting pan and place in the oven. Let cook for approximately 20 minutes per pound. Baste from time-to-time to keep moist. Once the turkey turns a golden color, especially around the leg area, cover lightly with tin foil and bake for the remaining time.

VEAL CUTLETS

Serves 6

2 pounds veal cutlets

4 large eggs

¼ cup pecorino romano, grated

¼ cup parmigiano, grated

2 cups seasoned breadcrumbs

4 parsley sprigs, chopped fine

½ tsp. garlic powder

½ tsp. black pepper

½ cup vegetable oil

½ cup olive oil

In a wide bowl, beat the eggs and mix with ¼ cup Parmigiano cheese. On a flat plate, combine the breadcrumbs, parsley, garlic powder, pepper and the ¼ cup Pecorino Romano cheese.

Dredge the veal pieces in the egg mixture. Allow excess egg batter to drip off, then carefully dredge into the breadcrumbs, coating both sides. Set coated veal scallops aside.

Combine the oils together. In a large sauté pan, heat half of the oil mixture over medium heat, (add the remaining oil as needed while frying). When the oil is very hot, but not smoking, carefully add the veal pieces to the pan. Brown each side, turning once, seasoning with salt and pepper as you turn. Continue to fry remaining pieces in batches until all cooked.

Lay veal pieces on a flat plate lined with a paper towel to absorb the extra oil. The cutlets can be covered lightly with tin foil until ready to serve.

VEAL MILANESE

Serves 6

prepared veal cutlets, pg. 132
1 medium red onion, chopped
¾ cup extra virgin olive oil
¼ cup balsamic vinegar
¼ tsp. sea salt

freshly ground black pepper
1 tbsp. dried oregano
½ pound mesclun or arugula
3 large tomatoes
2 lemons, cut into wedges

In a large bowl, prepare a tossed salad by combining the greens with the tomatoes.

*Do not put dressing on the salad until ready to serve.

In another smaller bowl, using a whisk, blend olive oil, balsamic vinegar, sea salt, black pepper and oregano, then add the onions and store at room temperature until ready to use.

Dress the salad with the dressing and toss, making sure the salad is coated. Plate each dish with a heap of salad, then place a veal cutlet on top. Serve with lemon wedges.

VEAL OR CHICKEN MARSALA

Serves 6

1 ½ lbs. veal or chicken cutlets
2 cups sliced white mushrooms
½ cup chicken broth
1 cup all-purpose flour

3 tbsp. butter
¾ cup marsala wine
1 cup vegetable oil
salt and pepper to taste

Prepare Cutlets:

Put ¼ cup of the oil in a medium sauté pan over medium heat. Add mushrooms, salt and pepper and sauté for about 5 minutes or until mushrooms have given off most of their juices. Then drain off any extra oil and add the chicken broth. Cook for another 5 minutes. Remove from heat and put it aside.

Season flour with salt, pepper and garlic powder. Heat the remaining oil in a large frying pan over medium heat. When the oil is very hot, quickly dredge each piece of meat in flour, shake off any extra flour and carefully place them in the pan. Brown each side, turning only once. Using a slotted metal spatula, remove the veal to a warm plate. Brown the remaining pieces.

Make Sauce:

When all the meat has been browned, drain the oil from the pan. Return the pan to medium heat and add the butter. After the butter has melted, return the meat pieces to the pan. Raise the heat and add the Marsala. Cook on high heat for 3 minutes. Add the mushrooms, salt and pepper. Remove the meat pieces only, and place on large serving platter. Bring the mushrooms and the sauce to a boil, scraping brown bits from the bottom. Pour the sauce over the meat and serve.

Basic Barbecue Rub
Best Barbecue Sauce
Florentine Herb Rub
Italian Rub
Mediterranean Herb Rub

Chimichurri Sauce
Red Curry Sauce
Teriyaki Sauce

Garlic, Lemon and Oil Marinade
Meat Marinade

Herbed Butter

Rubs and Sauces

BASIC BARBECUE RUB
Yields About 1 Cup

Rub it on ribs, steaks, chops, pork shoulder, chicken or anything you want to taste like American barbecue. Use 2 to 3 tsp. for pound of meat.

¼ cup firmly packed brown sugar

¼ cup sweet paprika

3 tbsp. black pepper

3 tbsp. coarse salt

1 tbsp. hickory-smoked salt or more coarse salt

2 tsp. garlic powder

2 tsp. onion powder

2 tsp. celery seeds

1 tsp. cayenne pepper

Combine all the ingredients in a mixing bowl or a Ziploc bag and mix well. Store rub in an airtight jar or plastic container. It will keep for 6-9 months.

BEST BARBECUE SAUCE
Yields About 2 ½ Cups

2 cups ketchup

¼ cup worcestershire sauce

¼ cup firmly packed brown sugar

2 tbsp. molasses

2 tbsp. prepared mustard

1 tbsp. of your favorite barbecue rub

2 tsp. liquid smoke

½ tsp. black pepper

Combine all the ingredients in a nonreactive saucepan and bring slowly to a boil over medium-high heat. Reduce the heat to medium and gently simmer the sauce until dark, thick and richly flavored, stirring frequently for 10 to 15 minutes. Transfer the sauce to a clean jar and store in the refrigerator. It will keep for several months.

FLORENTINE HERB RUB

8 fresh rosemary sprigs
10 fresh sage leaves
10 fresh thyme sprigs- no stems

1 clove garlic, peeled and crushed
4 tbsp. olive oil
1 tsp. salt
½ tsp. black pepper

Finely chop the rosemary, sage and thyme. Place in a bowl, then add the oil, garlic salt and pepper. Mix well and rub on steaks, chicken, or pork.

ITALIAN RUB

2 ½ tbsp. paprika
2 tbsp. salt
2 tbsp. garlic powder
1 tbsp. black pepper

1 tbsp. onion powder
1 tbsp. cayenne pepper
1 tbsp. oregano
1 tbsp. thyme

Whisk together all above ingredients. Store in a jar for up to 6 months.

MEDITERRANEAN HERB RUB
Yields About 1 Cup

Great rub for Lamb, Chicken, Fish and Seafood Use 2 to3 tsp. of rub per pound of meat, and rub all over meat.

3 tbsp. dried tarragon
3 tbsp. dried oregano
3 tbsp. dried dill
3 tbsp. dried thyme
3 tbsp. dried rosemary

3 tbsp. coarse salt
2 tbsp. lemon pepper (combine 1 tbsp. ground black pepper and 1 tbsp. of lemon zest)
1 tbsp. garlic flakes

Combine all ingredients in a bowl or in a zip lock bag. Store in an airtight jar or plastic container. It will keep for 6-9 months.

CHIMICHURRI SAUCE

1 cup flat leaf parsley leaves
3 garlic cloves
1 tsp. salt
2 tbsp. dried oregano
½ tsp. red pepper flakes

½ tsp. black pepper
¾ cup extra virgin olive oil
3 tbsp. sherry wine vinegar or red wine vinegar
3 tbsp. lemon juice

Place all the ingredients in a blender or food processor and pulse until well chopped. Chimichurri can be stored in the refrigerator for up to 1 month.

*Excellent on skirt steak, steak or chops.

RED CURRY SAUCE

1 can (15 oz.) coconut milk
2 tbsp. red curry paste

1 tbsp. brown sugar
1 tsp. fish sauce *optional

In a saucepan, bring the coconut milk to a simmer and add the red curry paste and the brown sugar (and the fish sauce if using it), bring to a boil and simmer for 5 minutes. Put aside until ready to use. Serve warm.

TERIYAKI SAUCE

3 cups saki   ¾ cup of soy sauce
6 tbsp. sugar   2 tsp. balsamic vinegar
4 tbsp. honey

Place all ingredients in a pan, cook and simmer over medium/low heat until sauce reduces and thickens.

*Store in refrigerator for up to 1 month

GARLIC, LEMON AND OIL MARINADE
(L'ansolio In Sicilian)

2 garlic cloves, chopped fine
1/3 cup extra virgin olive oil
juice of a half lemon
2 tsp. salt

½ tsp. black pepper
2 tbsp. dry oregano
4 tbsp. water

Place garlic and salt in a small bowl, and with a fork, crush the garlic into the salt to make a paste. Add the olive oil, stir, then add the lemon juice, oregano and pepper. Then add the water and stir well. Put to the side and keep at room temperature until ready to use.

*You can use this as a marinade or finishing sauce. Great on pork, steak and chicken. Tastes best when poured over hot grilled meat.

LONDON BROIL/MEAT MARINADE

¼ cup balsamic vinegar
¼ cup soy sauce
2 tbsp. worcestershire sauce
¼ cup olive oil

2 garlic cloves, crushed
1 tsp. rosemary
½ tsp. pepper
1 tsp. salt

Whisk together all above ingredients. Refrigerate for up to one month.

HERBED BUTTER
Makes 1 stick

2 sprigs rosemary

3 sprigs thyme

4 sprigs flat-leaf parsley

8 tbsp. butter, softened

Chop the rosemary, thyme and parsley fine and combine in a small bowl. Add the softened butter and using a fork blend the herbs and butter well. Once all is combined, form the butter into a long log and wrap in saran wrap and store in refrigerator until ready to use.

Great flavor for cooking or putting on potatoes, corn, lobster, meat, or anything you want to taste good.

Broccoli Rabe
Cocuzza (Italian Winter Squash)
Frittata of Asparagus
Green Peas
Grilled Asparagus
Mashed Potatoes
Olive Jarring
Stuffed Artichoke

Vegetables

Maria Francisco

BROCCOLI RABE
Serves 6

2 large bunches broccoli rabe	6 anchovy fillets, chopped
¼ cup extra virgin olive oil	4 cloves garlic, sliced
2 tbsp. butter	¼ tsp. black pepper

Remove any tough outer or damaged leaves. Cut off the thick stems up to the leaves and broccoli florets. Wash in the sink or large bowl with cold water, rinse.

In a deep saucepan, bring 2 quarts of water to a boil, add 1 tsp. salt and broccoli rabe. Cover and cook at a moderate boil until tender, about 10-15 minutes. Drain and set aside.

Put ¼ cup olive oil in large skillet with the chopped anchovies. Cook over medium heat, mashing the anchovies with a wooden spoon until they dissolve into a paste. Add garlic, sauté 2 min., then add the broccoli rabe, the pepper, and the 2 tbsp. butter. Turn the broccoli rabe into the anchovy paste as you sauté it lightly for 4-5 minutes. Taste and correct for salt (if the anchovies are very salty, none may be added).

COCUZZA
(Italian Winter Squash)
Serves 4

5 cups cocuzza,

¼ cup olive oil

4 cloves garlic, sliced

½ tsp. salt

¼ tsp. black pepper

Cut the cocuzza into 3" wedges. Using a potato peeler, carefully peel the hard outer skin off of the wedges and then slice them thin.

In a sauté pan, heat the oil over medium heat and add the garlic and sauté for a minute or so until garlic starts to turn golden. Add the cocuzza pieces and the salt and pepper and stir. Cover and simmer for 20 minutes, stirring occasionally.

FRITTATA OF ASPARAGUS
Serves 6

1 bunch of thin asparagus	2 tsp. salt
3 eggs, beaten	½ tsp. black pepper
¼ cup olive oil	

Cut ends off the asparagus (about 1"). In a large pot, bring 2" of water to a boil and 1 tsp. of salt, add the asparagus. Place lid on pot and let steam for 5 minutes. Drain the water and keep asparagus to the side.

In a large non-stick frying pan, heat the oil. When oil is hot, add the asparagus, salt and pepper and cook on medium low flame for 10 minutes. Stir, then add the egg mixture. Lower the flame to low and continue to cook until eggs are no longer runny. Then place a large dish, as big as the pan, on top and flip the frittata with the plate and return the uncooked side facing down, in pan. Let cook for 5 minutes more, then place on plate and cut into 6 wedges.

GREEN PEAS
Nonna Sara's Recipe
Serves 8

16 oz. bag frozen peas
¼ onion, chopped
¼ cup olive oil

1 tsp. salt
¼ tsp. black pepper

In a pot, add the oil, frozen peas, onion, salt and pepper. Stir well and cook on medium low flame for 20 minutes, stirring few times, so peas don't stick to the bottom.

GRILLED ASPARAGUS
Serves 6

1 bunch of asparagus

¼ cup of olive oil

1 tsp. of salt

½ tsp. black pepper

½ tsp. of garlic powder

Cut about 1" off the bottom (the wider part) of the asparagus. Rinse then dry with a paper towel.

Place asparagus in a baking pan then pour in the olive oil, sprinkle with the salt, pepper and garlic powder. Toss so that each asparagus gets coated with the oil.

You can either bake in oven at 350 degrees for 30 minutes or you can cook on the barbecue grill.

MASHED POTATOES

Serves 6

6 large potatoes	4 tbsp. butter
6 cups of water	¼ cup milk
1 tbsp. salt	

Remove skin and cut potatoes into 2 inch cubes.

Fill a large pot with water, add salt and potatoes so that potatoes are covered by 1 inch. Boil for 10 minutes or until potatoes are cooked.

Drain the potatoes, put them back in the pot and on a low flame, add the milk and the butter and with a wooden spoon or a masher, mash the potatoes and cook for a minute or two until butter has melted.

OLIVE JARRING
Nonna Sara's Recipe
Yields 14-16 jars
*The olives are typically harvested in early October

1 case (16lbs.) raw green olives

30 celery leaves

14 large garlic cloves, skin on

8-10 oz. salt

8 qt. water, room temperature

1 raw egg, room temperature

14 qt. mason jars with lids

2 large 6 or 8 qt. pots

On a cutting board, place an olive at a time, and crush the olive with a flat heavy stone or the bottom of a thick drink glass to crack the skin (keeping the pit intact), then place the cracked olives in large pot until filled 2/3 way up. Add some water to cover all the olives (you can place a flat large dish on top to keep the olives from floating to the top). Soak for 3 days, changing the water every morning. After the third day, drain all the water and put olives aside.

Prepare the Brine: Using a pot that can hold 8 quarts of liquid, fill the pot with the water and add the 8 oz. salt and, stirring slowly, dissolve the salt for a few minutes. *Once the salt is dissolved, you can test the salt concentration by submerging an egg. If the egg stands up vertically, there's enough salt. If not, add little more salt.

Assemble the jars: Fill them half way with the cracked olives, then add 1 garlic clove and 2 celery leaves. Add more olives to the top of the jar (they should fit snug). With a ladle, pour the salt brine to cover the olives and screw on tops. Olives are ready to eat around Thanksgiving, approximately 2 months after jarring. Store at room temperature for up to 3 years.

To dress the olives: Open the jar (it might fizz) and pour out the water, rinse, and drain well. Then add ¼ cup olive oil, 1/8 cup balsamic or red wine vinegar, black pepper, salt to taste, and oregano. Serve alone or in a salad.

STUFFED ARTICHOKE
Nonna Sara's Recipe
Serves 4

4 large artichokes

4 garlic cloves, peeled and halved

8 small chunks parmigiano

½ cup seasoned breadcrumbs

½ cup of olive oil

4 tsp. of salt

2 tsp. black pepper

Clean and prepare each artichoke by cutting off the end of the bottoms to make them flat, then peel off 2 rows of petals on the bottom of the artichoke. With a sharp knife, cut about 1½" off the top (pointy part) and with your hands, loosen and spread open the inside so it's ready for stuffing. Take 2 pieces of garlic and wedge down low into the artichoke in 2 places and take 2 pieces of cheese and do the same. Now that they are open, sprinkle each one with 1 tsp. salt and ½ tsp. pepper and some breadcrumbs. Drizzle tops with olive oil.

In a large pot place the stuffed artichokes, side by side making sure they are upright and snug. If they are not snug, place a small potato between them so they are. Then carefully, not to wet the inside stuffing, fill the pot with water until the water reaches 1 inch below the top of the artichokes. (You don't want the water to wash out your stuffing). Add 1 tbsp. of salt to the water and bring to a low boil on medium low heat. Place a lid on top and continue to cook for about 1 hour or until the artichokes are soft. Keep replacing water as needed, the water should always come 1" shy of the top of the artichokes.

*How to eat an artichoke: Starting with the outer leaves, one by one, put the leaf with the fleshy portion about ¾ of the way in the mouth, and with your teeth closed, pull the leaf through your teeth. As you get closer to the middle, the leaves will be thinner and you will be able to eat them whole. When you get to the bottom, remove the spikey filamentous part with a spoon and eat the heart, which is my daughter's favorite part. You may want to enjoy by dipping the leaves in melted butter.

Adult Pudding Shots
Banana Pudding with Vanilla Wafers
White Chocolate Cranberry Biscotti
Chocolate Covered Strawberries
Coquito
Coquito De Nutella
Cracker Candy
Cream Puffs
Flan de Coco
Funnel Cake
Limoncello
Lemon Cookies
Maria's House French Toast
Peach Cobbler
Peach Jam
Pumpkin Pie
Struffoli
Watermelon Mojitos
Zeppole

Desserts
and
Cocktails

Maria Francisco

ADULT PUDDING SHOTS
Serves 8

1 box chocolate instant pudding

1-1/4 cups cold milk

¼ cup vodka

½ cup baileys irish cream

8 oz. extra creamy cool whip

In a bowl, mix pudding and milk with an electric mixer (or whisk) for 2 minutes. Add the vodka and Baileys, stir until smooth, then add in the Cool Whip and stir well with a spoon.

Using a large spoon, place pudding into shot glasses and place in freezer until ready to serve.

BANANA PUDDING WITH VANILLA WAFERS

Serves 8

3 cups cold milk
2 pkg. vanilla instant pudding
vanilla wafers

3-4 medium bananas, sliced thin
whipped cream for topping

Pour milk into a large bowl, add the pudding mix and beat with a wire whisk for about 2 minutes until its thick and well blended. Let stand 5 minutes.

In a 2 quart serving bowl, or any bowl, (preferably a glass one), arrange the wafers on the bottom, placing them side-by-side, and then placing them standing up, 1 row high, on the sides of bowl. Then take the banana slices and place them on top of the wafers, also side by side and up 1 row on the sides of the bowl.

Pour the prepared pudding over the wafers and banana. Smooth out the top and refrigerate until ready to serve. Top with whipped cream.

WHITE CHOCOLATE –CRANBERRY BISCOTTI

Yields About 40 Biscotti

½ cup butter, softened

1 cup sugar

3 eggs

1 tsp. vanilla

3 cups all-purpose flour

1 tbsp. baking powder

¾ cup dried cranberries

¾ cup white chocolate chips

*can substitute cranberries and chocolate with nuts or other dried fruits

Preheat oven to 350 degrees.

In a large bowl, using a mixer (or a whisk), on low speed, mix cream butter and sugar until light and fluffy. Add the eggs, one a time, beating well after each addition. Beat in the vanilla. In another bowl, combine the flour with the baking powder. Gradually add a little at a time to the creamed mixture and mix well. Then stir in the cranberries and chocolate chips.

Divide the dough into 3 sections. Dust your hands and your work space with flour, then carefully lift each piece, forming it into a ball. Roll the dough out to 10"x 2" logs. Then carefully place the 3 logs on an ungreased, non-stick baking sheet and bake for 25 minutes.

Let cool and place on cutting board. Cut diagonally with a serrated knife into 1" pieces. Place cut-side down on an ungreased baking sheet. Bake again for 15-20 minutes or until golden brown. Let cool and store in an airtight container or tin.

CHOCOLATE COVERED STRAWBERRIES

1 lb. large, ripe strawberries
12 oz. chocolate morsels

½ tsp. coconut oil
sprinkles or crushed nuts

*The oil will help the spreading of the chocolate and will give them a nice shine. Can substitute coconut oil with vegetable oil.

Rinse strawberries, keeping the leaves on. Using a paper towel, pat dry thoroughly, otherwise your chocolate won't stick. Line the berries on a sheet of parchment paper or wax paper.

Place the chocolate and oil in a deep, small bowl and place in the microwave. Heat and stir morsels in 20-30 second intervals until the last chunks have melted and the chocolate is soft.

Then take the strawberries, one at a time, and holding by the leaves, dunk ¾ of the way up the berries into the chocolate. Gently shake off excess chocolate, then place carefully onto the parchment paper. At this point you can add sprinkles, crushed nuts, or anything you'd like.

Place in refrigerator to harden for at least 20 minutes. Keep them refrigerated until ready to serve.

Maria Francisco

COQUITO
(Puerto Rican Eggnog)

2 egg yolks, whisked

24 oz. condensed milk

2 cups coconut milk

12 oz. heavy cream

½ tsp. cinnamon

¼ tsp. nutmeg

2 cups white rum

Stir all ingredients with a whisk. Ladle eggnog into bottles and keep refrigerated.

COQUITO DE NUTELLA

4 cans evaporated milk

2 cans condensed milk

2 cans coconut milk

2 cans coconut cream

½ cup nutella

4 cups white rum

1 tsp. cinnamon

1 tsp. vanilla

Pour all ingredients in a blender and mix well. Pour into bottles and refrigerate. Serve cold

CRACKER CANDY

1 sleeve of saltine crackers

1 cup butter

1 cup plus 2 tbsp. brown sugar

1 cup pecans, crushed

1 bag chocolate morsels

Preheat oven to 350 degrees

Line a baking sheet with parchment paper or tin foil sprayed with nonstick spray. Layer the crackers side-by-side until the whole tray is covered with saltine crackers.

In a pot over medium low flame, melt butter and sugar and cook, stirring until it comes to a boil. Boil for 3 minutes, stirring constantly. Pour mixture over crackers and spread evenly. Bake for 5 minutes, remove from the oven and sprinkle the chocolate morsels over the entire tray. Cover with tin foil for few minutes (to soften chocolate), then spread the chocolate evenly. Sprinkle with pecans. Place in the freezer for 10 minutes, then break off into pieces.

CREAM PUFFS
Zizi Carmela's Recipe
Paul's Favorite
Serves 8

1 cup water
1 stick unsalted butter
pinch of salt

1 cup flour
4 eggs
2 pkgs. vanilla instant pudding

Prepare the vanilla pudding according to the instructions on the box and refrigerate for at least an hour before using.

Preheat oven to 425 degrees.

Prepare a 10x15 baking pan by lining the bottom with parchment paper or by coating the bottom with butter and dusting with flour.

In a large pot, pour the water, add the butter, pinch of salt and bring to a boil. Remove from heat and add the flour to the pan, stirring until it forms a ball. Incorporate the eggs, one at a time, with an electric hand mixer until all is well-mixed.

Using a large spoon, scoop out a heaping spoonful of the dough. Using your index finger, remove the dough off the spoon (in round shapes) and place on baking pan a few inches in between each other. Place in the oven and bake at 425 degrees for 10 minutes, then reduce heat to 350 degrees for the remaining 15-20 minutes. Cream puffs are done when they are puffed and a golden color. Remove from heat and let cool.

Cut each cream puff in half, separating the top from the bottom. Remove the top part and spoon a heaping tbsp. of vanilla pudding in the center. Place the top back and before serving, dust with powdered sugar.

*If you dust the sugar on before serving and refrigerate, the sugar will melt and cause your cream puffs to be soggy.

FLAN DE COCO
(Coconut Flan)
Serves 6

1 cup granulated sugar

¼ cup water

4 eggs

7.5 oz. cream of coconut

14 oz. sweetened condensed milk

12 oz. evaporated milk

½ tsp. vanilla

Preheat oven to 350 degrees.

Heat a small pot over medium low heat. Add the sugar and water, stirring until the sugar has melted and has turned into a golden liquid caramel, (careful not to overcook or caramel will turn dark brown and burn). Quickly pour into a medium pan or pie dish and swirl around so that the caramel coats the bottom of the pan.

In a blender, combine eggs, cream of coconut, evaporated milk, sweetened condensed milk and vanilla. Blend for 1 minute. Put aside.

The flan will cook in the oven in a water bath. To make the water bath, pull out the oven rack and place the large pan on it. Place the medium flan pan in the center of the larger pan. Pour the mixture in the medium pan over the caramel. With a pitcher, pour water into the larger pan, surrounding the flan pan, until water reaches half way. Then carefully push the rack in and bake for 1hr. 15 minutes to 1 hr. 30 minutes.

Carefully remove from the oven and the water bath and let sit at room temperature for an hour. Then refrigerate overnight or for several hours before serving.

Using a knife, loosen along the outer wall between the pan and the flan. Place a large flat serving dish over the pan, then carefully flip over so to release the flan gently.

FUNNEL CAKE
Serves 8

3 cups all-purpose flour

¼ tsp. salt

½ tsp. baking soda

¼ cup sugar

3 tsp. baking powder

2 eggs

1 cup milk

1 cup water

confectioner's sugar for dusting

In a large bowl, beat eggs and add vanilla, milk and water until well-blended. In another bowl, whisk the flour, salt, baking soda, sugar and baking powder; beat into the egg mixture until smooth. In an electric skillet or deep fryer, heat oil to 375 degrees. *Test with a spoon full of mixture to make sure oil is hot enough. The batter should turn a golden-brown.

Cover the bottom of a funnel spout with your finger; ladle a ½ cup of the batter at a time to the funnel. Holding the funnel several inches above the oil, release your finger and move the funnel in a spiral motion until all the batter is released, scraping with a rubber spatula if needed.

Fry 2 minutes on each side or until golden brown. Drain on paper towels. Dust with confectioners' sugar, serve warm.

LIMONCELLO

zest of 20 lemons, *organic
(use zester or peeler, yellow zest only, no flesh)

2 fifth bottles (750 ml each) pure grain alcohol
  or vodka

In a large stainless steel pot or glass container, soak the lemon zest and pure grain alcohol. Cover with a lid for 10 days.

After 10 days, prepare sugar water* and add to the pot, mix well and refrigerate for 24 hours. Using a cheesecloth, strain liquid into bottles, discard lemon rinds, and store in freezer. Serve cold.

Sugar Water:

2 quarts water

6 cups sugar

Dissolve the sugar in water over medium heat (approximately 15 minutes). Let cool.

LEMON COOKIES

Nonna Sara Recipe

For the cookie recipe:

4 cups flour

4 medium eggs

4 tsp. baking powder

1 tbsp. vanilla extract

1 cup sugar

1 cup Crisco

For the sugar glaze coating:

1 box of granulated sugar

4 tbsp. of milk

1 tsp. lemon extract

In a large bowl, blend the Crisco and flour with your hands. In a separate bowl, beat the eggs, vanilla and the sugar, then add to the flour mixture along with the baking powder. Mix well with your hands. Once the dough is of cookie consistency, shape into 3" logs and place on non-stick baking pan or on parchment paper.

Bake 350 degrees for about 40 minutes until done. Let cool

In a large bowl, combine the sugar with the milk and the lemon extract until silky consistency, not too runny. After cookies have cooled, dunk them in the bowl and coat them with the glaze. Place on wax paper to dry. Store in the refrigerator.

MARIA'S HOUSE FRENCH TOAST
Serves 8

½ cup chopped pecans

¼ cup golden raisins

4 large apples (sliced)

1 ½ cups milk

5 eggs

1 tsp. vanilla

1/4 tsp. cinnamon

thick-sliced white bread

*Great especially on the Holidays, prepare the night before.

In a 9"x13" pan, pour the syrup mixture on the bottom, sprinkle with the chopped pecans, raisins, then place a layer of the apple slices and layer of the thick bread.

Mix together in a bowl, milk, eggs, and vanilla, then pour over bread. Sprinkle with cinnamon. Cover with foil and refrigerate overnight. Bake uncovered at 350 degrees for 40 minutes.

For Syrup:

½ cup brown sugar

½ cup butter

2 tbsp. dark or light corn syrup

Simmer together for 3 minutes, keep warm.

PEACH COBBLER

Serves 4

For the Peach Filling:

4 cups fresh peach slices (peeled and cut into thin wedges)

1 cup sugar

1 tbsp. fresh lemon juice

1 tsp. cornstarch

ground cinnamon or nutmeg

For the Cake Batter:

1 cup all-purpose flour

1 cup sugar

1 tbsp. baking powder

½ tsp. salt

½ cup unsalted butter

1 cup milk

Preheat the oven to 375 degrees.

Melt butter in a 13"x9" baking dish.

In a bowl, combine the flour, sugar, baking powder and salt, then add the milk. Stir until dry ingredients are moist. Pour over the butter and do not stir.

In a saucepan, bring 1 cup sugar, peach slices, lemon juice and cornstarch to a boil over high heat, stirring constantly for a few minutes. Pour over the batter (do not stir). Sprinkle with cinnamon, if desired, and bake for 40-45 minutes until golden brown. Let cool for 5 minutes, then serve warm with vanilla ice cream.

PEACH JAM

4 pounds ripe peaches (4 ½ cups)   1 box pectin

3 cups sugar   small mason jars

2 tbsp. fresh lemon juice

Peel and finely chop the peaches and place in a large pot. Add the lemon juice and ¼ cup of the sugar and mix with pectin. Stir continuously on high flame until "rolling bubbles" start. (Bubbles that don't stop after you stir).
Add the rest of the sugar. Bring back to rolling bubbles and continue stirring for 1 minute. Turn off the flame and remove from heat.

Prepare the water bath using a large canner or pot with a rack on the bottom. Fill 1/3 way up with water; it should cover the tops of the jars by 1". Heat water until hot, but not boiling. Alternately, you can warm your jars in the oven on very low heat or in your dishwasher. *If jars are cold, they might crack when you pour in the hot jam.

Fill the warm jars leaving 1 ¼" for head space, then wipe the rims clean and place your lids tightly. Carefully place the jars on the rack in the canner. The rack will keep the jars off the bottom and from hitting each other. The water needs to flow freely around each jar. Add hot water if needed until the jars are covered by at least 1 inch. Cover and come to a full boil for 20 minutes. Remove jars from hot water and place, not touching one another, on a dishtowel. Cover with another dishtowel and let cool overnight. Seal on the caps, which should be indented when the jars cool.

Jam can be stored for up to 2 years.

PUMPKIN PIE

2 cups mashed, freshly cooked pumpkin

1 (12oz.) evaporated milk

2 eggs beaten

¾ cups brown sugar

½ tsp. cinnamon

½ tsp. grated ginger

½ tsp. nutmeg

½ tsp. salt

Heat oven to 400 degrees

Halve and peel a small pumpkin and cut into chunks. Boil the chunks in 2 inches of water, cover and simmer for 30 minutes.

Drain, cool, mash with potato masher. Remove any liquid. With mixer, beat pumpkin with evaporated milk, eggs, brown sugar, cinnamon, ginger, nutmeg and salt.

Pour into a prepared crust pie plate and bake for 45 minutes.

STRUFFOLI
(Sicilian Honey Balls)

2 cups flour	3 large eggs
1 large lemon, zested	1 tsp. pure vanilla extract
½ large orange, zested	vegetable or canola oil for frying
3 tbsp. sugar	1 cup honey
½ tsp. salt	½ cup sugar
¼ tsp. baking powder	1 tbsp. lemon juice
½ stick butter, softened	nonpareil sprinkles for decoration

In the bowl of a food processor or blender, pulse together 2 cups of flour, lemon zest, orange zest, sugar, salt, and baking powder. Add the ½ inch pieces of butter. Pulse until the mixture resembles a coarse meal. Add the eggs and vanilla. Pulse until the mixture forms into a ball. Wrap the dough in plastic wrap and refrigerate for 30 minutes.

Cut the dough into 4 equal-sized pieces. On a lightly floured surface, roll out each piece of dough until it forms a ½ inch thick log. Cut each log into ½ inch pieces of dough. Lightly dredge the dough balls in flour, shaking off any excess. In a large heavy-bottomed saucepan, pour enough oil to fill the pan just about a third of the way. Heat over medium heat until the oil reaches 375 degrees. If you don't have a thermometer to determine heat, test a ball to make sure oil is hot enough. In batches, (careful not to overcrowd, this will cause oil to bubble over), fry the dough until lightly golden, about 2 to 3 minutes. Transfer to a paper towel-lined plate to drain.

In a large saucepan, combine the honey, sugar and lemon juice over medium heat. Bring to a boil and cook, stirring occasionally, until the sugar dissolves, about 3 minutes. Remove the pan from the heat. Add the fried dough balls and stir until all balls are coated in the honey. Allow the mixture to cool in the pan for 2 minutes. Using a large spoon or damp hands, arrange struffoli on a platter. Decorate with sprinkles.

WATERMELON MOJITOS

4 cups watermelon

½ cup fresh lime juice

¼ cup packed mint leaves

2 cups white rum

¼ cup agave syrup

Cube and seed the watermelon. In batches, use a blender to puree watermelon pieces, lime juice and mint until smooth. Strain into a pitcher, then add rum and syrup. Stir to mix well and refrigerate.

Agave can be replaced with ½ cup simple syrup. Combine ½ cup water and ½ cup sugar; cook over low heat until sugar dissolves. Let cool

ZEPPOLE
(Sicilian Style)
Nonna Sara's Recipe
Makes a Full Tray

6 eggs
1 pound ricotta
2 tbsp. vanilla extract

2 cups of presto flour
vegetable oil for frying

Place eggs in a bowl and lightly blend with electric mixer, then add the vanilla, the ricotta and the flour. Mix well, put to side.

In a deep pan, pour oil about 1/3 way up. Heat the oil, and when it's hot, drop a heaping tbsp. of the mixture into the pan. let stand then when it floats to the top, flip it over. Do not overcrowd them or they will stick together. When golden on both sides, remove with a slotted spoon and place on paper towels.

When they are all done, let cool then place on tray. Sprinkle with powdered sugar right before serving, otherwise the sugar will get wet and absorbed.

ABOUT THE AUTHOR

Maria Francisco, born Lilla Maria Territo in Ribera, Sicily, is a loving wife and mother of two happy children. She enjoys nothing more than playing a range of music from Andrea Boccelli or reggaeton while cooking in the kitchen, always with a glass of red wine in one hand.

Maria feels that food is the bond that brings people together. It provides not only physical, but spiritual and emotional nourishment. Good food is the way to everyone's heart.

" When life gives you lemons, make limoncello." - Anonymous

Made in the USA
Middletown, DE
13 January 2020